# CARING
## FOR YOUR
# PASTOR

### Helping God's Servant
### to Minister with Joy

## lorna dobson

kregel
PUBLICATIONS

Grand Rapids, MI 49501

*Caring for Your Pastor: Helping God's Servant to Minister with Joy*

© 2001 by Lorna Dobson

Published by Kregel Publications, a division of Kregel, Inc., P.O. Box 2607, Grand Rapids, MI 49501. Kregel Publications provides trusted, biblical publications for Christian growth and service. For more information about Kregel Publications, visit our Web site: www.kregel.com.

Cover and Book Design: John M. Lucas

**Library of Congress Cataloging-in-Publication Data**
Dobson, Lorna
    Caring for your pastor: helping God's servant to minister with joy / by Lorna Dobson
        p. cm.
Includes bibliographical references.
        1. Clergy—Office. 2. Church controversies. 3. Interpersonal relations—Religious aspects—Christianity. 4. Church etiquette. I. Title.
BV660.3 .D63      2001       253'.2—dc21       2001029021

ISBN 0-8254-2461-5                               CIP

Printed in the United States of America

1  2  3  4  5 / 05  04  03  02  01

# CONTENTS

# FOREWORD

I have long been dismayed by seeing well-meaning Christians relating so poorly to their pastor. As a Christian bookstore owner for more than twenty years, I attempted to befriend pastors who often had nowhere else to turn during difficult times in their ministry. As a result, many of my closest friends are ministers. How I would have loved to have had this resource to share with their church members! Lorna Dobson has given us who are the sheep a wonderfully practical and common-sense guide to loving and supporting those whom God has given us as our church's shepherd. It should be required reading for every Christian!

—Jim Reimann, editor, Updated Editions of *Streams in the Desert* and *My Utmost for His Highest*

# INTRODUCTION

As a teenager, I observed a split in my church that divided families and ended friendships. I never knew the whole story, but sin was evident in both the alleged cause for the split and in the way it was handled. The difficulties encountered within the church body demonstrated a failure of the test God periodically gives to see if we "love one another deeply" (1 Peter 1:22).

A few years later, I lived thousands of miles from my home with a young missionary couple and a small group of students and leaders. A second missionary group worked in another town. Our group made house-to-house visits in preparation for the start-up of a local church. The joy of seeing people trust Christ as Savior in Bible clubs, Sunday school, and prison ministry was often overshadowed by tension between the two missionary groups. Rules had been made by agencies that prevented us from associating with those other believers whose goal was the same as ours: making disciples, baptizing, and teaching obedience to God's commands (Matt. 28:18–20). I sensed that something was wrong with "the picture," since the rules were not based on theological differences but on matters of preference and practice.

I was confused because of the contradiction. I was not allowed to meet with and enjoy the company of people whom the Bible told me to love deeply. Several years ago, one of our team members visited the church that had been planted. She told me that the same concept of exclusivity was ingrained in the people and is still evident, even though the church planter left long ago. Today, as a pastor's wife with thirty-three years of active Christian ministry behind me, I still ponder with sadness these two situations. I have observed and discussed many ministry challenges, both with laypeople and with those called to full-time ministry. While not all challenges are related to moral failures or to rules and preferences, as in the stories above, the stresses and tensions that challenges create directly impact the relationship between ministers and those they serve. Those stresses and tensions eventually will manifest themselves—sometimes in spiritual immaturity, sometimes even in sinful behavior and attitudes. This results in heartache between believers—between those who should manifest love toward each other in a way that attracts the unbelieving world to the "good news" we long to share.

But there is another reason to resolve discord among believers: "so that their work will be a joy" (Heb. 13:17). Whose work? The leaders—those who teach us the Word of God (v. 7). And what will give the leaders joy? The obedience and submission (v. 17) of followers as we voluntarily bow to the Father in deference, in awe, and in total commitment (12:9).

Oh—this submission is hard! Giving up our will to His will is difficult, even for those who are redeemed and who yield their lives to Him. Our wills often follow our desires, even when we know that giving up and giving in are what it takes to experience true freedom in Christ. I, too, am always learning to submit to authority. While I consider myself to be in full-time ministry, as an unpaid volunteer worker I frequently must submit to others' authority—it goes with the territory.

*Authority* is a term I've balked at all my life (although outwardly, I often appear compliant), and I sense that many other well-meaning believers experience the same struggle. As soon as we surrender one area and give God the lead, He gently shows us another that needs repentance, one that we must transform and then conform to His will.

It is easy to become discouraged, but refusing to submit often develops into situations and attitudes that are not joy-giving for ministry leaders. While ministry leaders are accountable to God (as well as to trusted godly Christian brothers and sisters), those under that leadership have a responsibility not to hinder God's work and take joy from their leaders' service.

For me, every thought, every decision, every action must be focused on Christ and led by His Spirit. Pure joy is the fruit of that surrender, and my joy as a follower of Christ, experienced in a life of obedience, will be a source of joy to those in leadership over me, including my own husband.

The same principle applies to you, the reader, and your relationship with your pastor. Perhaps you think that your life, your decision whether or not to obey the Lord, matters to no one but you and your immediate family. But you play a part in the lives of the people who lead you. You have a responsibility to know and obey the Word of God, just as your pastor and church leadership do. You (and I) are on the pathway to conforming to the image of Christ.

It is this conformity to Christ that I ponder whenever I hear of the stress, tension, difficulties, and sorrows that people of faith experience in ministering to each other. The surrendered will of the person doing the work of the ministry, and the surrendered will of the person being ministered to, together should result in joy. But it is only by looking within our hearts, detecting what needs to be submitted to God and obeying what we learn from His Word, that we, as servants, live up to our responsibility—contributing to the joy that ministers should feel in fulfilling their call to the work of the Lord. Carrying out this responsibility to our ministers is evidence that we are fulfilling the "whole duty of man," which is to "fear God and keep his commandments" (Eccl. 12:13).

When I began writing this book, I had no intention of trying to influence church attenders to become members. However, as this project comes to an end, I realize that the issues of obedience and submission are difficult to address when people are doing everything they can to leave all their options open.

A large number of American adults are hesitant to make commitments in many areas of life. Commitment to the local church is no exception. They want to test the water to see if the temperature is comfortable. Twenty years ago, plunging into church membership was an exciting, but common, event. Today, however, it is not uncommon for people to spend their lives on the "dock" (which looks much like a pew), dipping a big toe into the water (minimal church participation), but never diving into the full commitment it takes to become a member. If the church people attend doesn't suit their comfort zone, they'll simply test the water of another church.

As a pastor's wife I have observed the frustration this mindset causes both paid and volunteer church staff. With time, it becomes increasingly difficult to pour your heart into people who refuse to settle down and serve. For those readers who have decided not to decide, I challenge you to prayerfully consider your response to the command to "obey and submit" given in Hebrews 13:7.

This book addresses the everyday, practical interactions between believers—whether these believers are inactive or active laypersons, paid ministry staff in churches, or paid staff in parachurch ministries—and illustrates ways in which these interactions can impede or facilitate a leader's ability to serve with joy. The book also illustrates ways to prevent and/or rectify unpleasant interactions and situations. Because I am a pastor's wife, my illustrations often involve my husband. But all persons in ministry positions deal with similar challenges. The principles discussed can be translated to your own circumstances. Some illustrations have been changed slightly to protect the identity of individuals; other stories are told with the permission of the people involved.

Perhaps my openness about our lives and the lives of others in ministry will enlighten and inspire readers, showing them practical ways to develop a relationship of mutual responsibility and respect with their pastor.

Throughout the book there are prayer suggestions that readers can use to uplift their ministers on a daily basis and in the various seasons of their lives.

As this book goes to press, my family and I are again reminded of the importance of other believers' prayers on our behalf. Early in 2000, my husband began having muscle twitches in his arms. Testing in late fall of that year resulted in a probable diagnosis of the motor-neuron disease ALS (Lou Gehrig's Disease), with muscle deterioration in Ed's right hand and arm. Another round of tests in early 2001 showed no further progression of the disease, and we are very thankful that symptoms have still only been detected in one limb, which remains functional. During these days of medical uncertainty, we are literally deluged with calls, cards, creative forms of encouragement, and promises of prayer.

We are grateful for the army of praying people who lift Ed up to the throne of God. I also have been praying that Christians would pray more for hurting, suffering brothers and sisters and their caregivers, and begin to lavish more of the love on one another that God has lavished upon us.

As we look at our relationships with fellow believers, let us take time to be still and to conform our hearts and lives to the image of Christ, who is the image of the invisible God. Does our walk bring joy to Him? Do we allow those in ministry leadership the freedom to serve with joy? Or, rather, do we hamper them with our willfulness and make their journey seem like drudgery? Once we have learned, through scriptural principles, the true path of joy—may the latter never be so.

*Section 1*

# UNDERSTANDING YOUR PASTOR

---

*Chapter 1*

---

# WHAT DO PASTORS DO?

"I'd like to have lunch with Pastor Zeal," Jim told his wife, Sarah, on the way home from church, "but he's so busy. I don't want to bother him. Maybe we should invite him and his whole family to dinner, instead."

"Oh heavens," Sarah moaned. "I'd never get the house clean enough . . . and what would I cook? Can we paint the dining room first?"

"I've been attending this church for three months," Nancy said, as she walked into church with her friend, "and I'm just dying to meet the pastor. But I've avoided him at the door because I don't know what to say."

"There's the pastor's wife," Millie pointed out to her mother, as they watched Mrs. Star walk into the grocery store. "I wonder if she's going to buy angel food cake!" They laughed at their little joke.

"I drove past the golf course yesterday," Bob told his brother, as they jogged together. "I saw Pastor Perk carrying his clubs. I'd like to golf with him sometime, but maybe he doesn't want to be with church members on his day off—and he's probably too busy the rest of the week. I know he wouldn't play with us on Sunday!"

To some church members, a pastor is a robed, eloquent

speaker behind the pulpit, and they are happy to leave him there. If you have ever wanted to know your pastor more personally, however, you may have participated in a conversation like those above. You wouldn't be the first. I've heard all the above in various forms. Some people freeze when the minister enters the room, fearing they might say something unsacred that would offend. Other than engaging in polite small talk, they just don't know what to say, so they attend church for many years, feeling unconnected and awkward around the pastor.

That is not the case, however, for all church members. Many people break the ice by inviting several couples when they have the pastor and spouse for dinner. Others get to know the pastor through activities that their children and the pastor's kids have in common. Some host a spur-of-the-moment barbecue when they happen to catch the minister's family at a time when everyone is free for a couple of hours.

Whether or not members have experienced any of these situations, they may have wondered from a distance what their pastor is really like. Reasons such as age differences or lack of time might have inhibited their desire to form a personal relationship with the pastor. Other people simply may not have felt a need to communicate directly with their ministers. "Maybe someday," they think. Waiting for someday, though, may not be the best plan.

Clark, for example, had received an ominous medical report, and he made an appointment to see my husband, Ed. Clark had been a leader in the church for many years, and his children and grandchildren were members. But, for the first time in his life, he desired to have a personal conversation with a pastor. Though Clark felt assured of his destiny in heaven, it was time to settle other important matters. Talking to the minister seemed the right thing to do as Clark now faced his limited time on earth. By God's grace, Clark lived another five years, and through that first serious conversation with Ed the door was opened for a closeness that quickly developed into a loving bond between the two of them.

Not all church members wait until they are facing death before initiating a friendship with their minister. Many people consider the pastor their teacher, guide, mentor, and even their friend. If so, asking their pastor questions may come naturally. When members can obtain guidance from their pastor in smaller things, or if they can come to know the personal side of the one who teaches them truth, then the door is often opened for them to trust on a deeper level when they have significant needs. Some church members, however, feel intimidated by the pastor's position. They have been taught to be respectful, and their respect for a pastor's calling prevents them from seeing that ministers are real people. Many want to say an encouraging word but don't want to sound trite, so they say nothing. Others have no idea what is or is not an appropriate time to call, write, or speak to their minister, because they do not understand what ministers and their families do apart from what members see on Sundays. As a pastor's wife, I hope to share some insights into the lives of ministry families and, by doing so, remove much of the mystery.

Let me first say that I am thankful to God for placing Ed and me in ministry together nearly twenty-nine years ago. We have been in a position to help others, to share the good news of God's love and the gift of salvation through His Son, to teach people, and to encourage them in their faith. But, in turn, Christians have taught us so much by their abiding walk with the Lord. We have so often been encouraged by godly people who do thoughtful things for us, and who love us in ways that refuel our ministry.

Like the vast majority of both lay and professional ministers, we didn't go into ministry for strokes. But I have to admit that little kindnesses help, especially if we are feeling bombarded with criticism or when we are experiencing the rigors of assisting and counseling troubled people. We appreciate people who understand that we, too, continue to grow and learn in our walk with the Lord, and that we struggle with our weaknesses. Like you and like the apostle Paul, we fight the continuous war between our spirits and the desires of our bodies (Rom. 7:15–23). Not all of ministry life is tough, of course. God has abundantly blessed us with a great measure of joy in our ministry together and our growing relationship with Christ. But much of ministry life *is* difficult, because ministers spend a significant amount of time with people who are going through stressful periods. That part never ends.

Many church members observe and understand the dynamics of ministry. Because they do, they communicate with, support, and assist their ministers. It is unfortunate, however, that a great number do not. Let me illustrate. I have attended retreats for ministry couples or pastors' wives. Teary-eyed, these couples or wives often thank the retreat leaders because they have found notes or flowers or fruit baskets in their rooms. They are touched, saying that no one has ever treated them with such kindness. At one retreat, a hospitality room was set up for the women to exchange clothes and accessories. Some women went away with new wardrobes, and for the first time in their ministries had felt truly cared for.

In order to understand how to support ministers, it might be helpful to first understand what ministers do.

In a discussion with one young man, I referred to my husband's daily routine as his *occupation*. "But what does he *do?*" the young man asked. "I thought that ministering was a calling. Something that is holy and divine. I've never asked anyone before, but is what your husband does his *job?* Does he get paid? How does he get paid? Per sermon, or like every two weeks?"

I chuckled inwardly, thinking of the criteria a church board might use to tabulate the worth of each sermon. But I replied, "Jesus said workers in the Lord's harvest deserve their wages"

(Luke 10:7). The apostle Paul repeated those words in his letter to Timothy, and he added that the "elders who direct the affairs of the church well are worthy of double honor, *especially those whose work is preaching and teaching*" (1 Tim. 5:17–18, emphasis added).

In the early church (Acts 6:1–4) the apostles soon realized they could not do everything that was needed in ministering to people. Therefore, they chose mature, Spirit-filled men who could distribute food (that is, administrate), while they gave their "attention to prayer and the ministry of the word." That biblical model is followed today. Lay and staff leadership share the ministry load so that the pastor may spend significant time in prayer and in preparation for the delivery of the message.

The "ministry of the word" may include, however, more than preaching a sermon. Ministering the Word also means being a living example to people in every opportunity that arises for teaching the gospel. According to Ephesians, apostles, prophets, evangelists, pastors, and teachers were "to prepare God's people for works of service, so that the body of Christ may be built up until we all reach unity in the faith and in the knowledge of the Son of God and become mature, attaining to the whole measure of the fullness of Christ" (4:12–13).

As for the young man's question, "What does a pastor *do?*"—it is likely that other people wonder how pastors spend their days. Some may have the notion that ministers read the Bible all day and think of something to say about it on Sundays. Few people realize the planning and research that is involved in handling the Word of God so as to convey, through the power of the Holy Spirit, its truth in love and in ways that apply to the listeners' lives. It is common knowledge that pastors may make a visit now and then, may drop in on someone at the hospital, do a few funerals and weddings, make a few phone calls, and offer a prayer at a civic event. But other than that, the way they spend their time is a mystery to many people in the congregation.

I could create a table of how Ed spends his time, but often a minister's daily schedule is not lived out as planned. Flexibility is key, since the job demands that the pastor be available at any time to minister to people in crisis. Needless to say, the planned schedule of a pastor does not show Sunday as a day of rest. Pastors spend Sundays doing their jobs—preaching and leading prayer, talking to parishioners, attending to the myriad details that go into a day of services. Ed uses Thursday as his day off, a day in which he spends time with his family, perhaps enjoying a game of golf, or attending one of the children's activities. In the other five days of the week, Ed might plan to spend three mornings doing office work and studying. Most weekdays he has lunch appointments, and afternoons are occupied by more appointments, such as meetings with engaged couples, nonchurch related committee meetings, and staff meetings. In the evening, Ed might lead a Bible study group or attend the church board meeting. Fridays might include a wedding. Saturday night he speaks on rotation with an associate pastor for our nontraditional service; then later in the evening Ed reads through his notes for the next day's services. That is Ed's *planned* schedule for the week.

His actual schedule is often somewhat different. The mornings he planned to spend in the office or in study may be interrupted by walk-in visitors or phone calls. He might try to write a chapter or two for a book he is working on. The planned afternoon and evening schedule must accommodate telephone calls (he might speak to five or six people on the phone after supper), the studying that he did not get done in the morning, a speaking engagement at one of the church's special group meetings, some visits to bereaved members, or a counseling session with a person who wishes to make a decision for the Lord.

Then there are funerals, which often turn neatly planned days upside down. Ed makes himself available to the bereaved family from the time their loved one dies until interment, and this is true of many pastors. In some cases his presence may not be needed much until the day of the funeral, but in others he spends many hours with the family. He always tries to learn as much as possible about the loved one so he can personalize the service as well as aid the family in the grieving process.

This "job description" will certainly not be exactly the same for all men and women in ministry. Some clergy step up to the pulpit on Saturdays instead of Sundays, and often each week is entirely different from the one that went before. Some pastors may spend much of their time counseling, while others may spend several days a week visiting people in their homes or in the hospital. All pastors I have ever known attend board meetings. Some give priority to sermon preparation. Others try to avoid scheduling appointments, knowing that they are often unexpectedly called away and will disappoint people.

Religions and denominations vary widely, even within a particular geographic region. Each pastor is unique in style and belief. Church members often compare notes about their churches with friends and relatives who live in other cities or states. In today's mobile society, people who are relocating are often already knowledgeable about churches in their new communities. With informed insight into a minister's schedule and priorities, members can avoid misunderstandings and make good choices in where they attend church.

# Chapter 2

# WHY BECOME A PASTOR?

It is not my purpose to explore the ways in which people discover, answer, or surrender to God's call to ministry. Suffice it to say that God does call people at various times in their lives and under different circumstances. Consider for example the call of the prophet Isaiah, which came in a vision and is recorded in Isaiah 6. The story of the boy Samuel's call from God and his answer to it, found in 1 Samuel 3, had a profound impact on a young boy named Billy Hybels, who asked his schoolteacher if God still spoke to little boys. Her positive answer kept him listening for God's voice throughout his life. Bill Hybels founded Willow Creek Church near Chicago, and it now influences worldwide ministry.

Though the Scripture passages quoted in the following paragraphs describe a pastor and do not specifically show how to determine if someone has the call, they do give insights into the reasons clergy answer that call.

The word *pastor* comes from a Latin word that means shepherding—devotion to guiding the flock—a term closely parallel to the one used in Psalm 23:1 where the Lord is described as being our Shepherd. The "Sovereign Lord . . . tends his flock like a shepherd: He gathers the lambs in his arms and carries them close to his heart; he gently leads those that have young" (Isa. 40:10–11). In the New Testament, Jesus refers to Himself as the "good shepherd" (John 10:14).

In the practice of keeping livestock, the shepherd's job is to give TLC (tender loving care). While the pastor feeds the lambs, caring tenderly for the young, the feeble, and the abandoned, at the same time he leads the whole flock to pastures and guides the mature ones to feed themselves. Even though many of the sheep can eat by themselves, they remain dependent on the leadership of the shepherd to keep the flock together and protect it from enemies. We, as Christians, can feed on the Word of God alone, and we are always dependent on Christ, the Chief Shepherd, who "is the head of the body, the church" (Col. 1:18). Yet we need the leadership of our earthly caregiver—the pastor—sometimes referred to as the "undershepherd."

Looking back, then, at the questions raised by the young man at the opening of this section—is what pastors do a divine and holy calling? The apostle Paul said that he was "compelled to preach. Woe to me if I do not preach the gospel" (1 Cor. 9:16). Older, godly people often tell young people who are considering ministry, "If you can do anything else and be content, do it. But if you cannot keep from it, God is calling you."

Ed felt called to preach before he and I met, so that matter was settled before we got married. The test for us as to how that call would be carried out came when we were newlyweds in 1972. Ed had been asked to consider taking a job as dean of men in a new Christian school called Liberty Baptist College in Lynchburg, Virginia. Ed told Pastor Jerry Falwell, the founder, that he would work there as long as he would be allowed to preach whenever and wherever opportunities arose. If he could not preach, he would have to quit working at the school. Dr. Falwell agreed, and for nearly fifteen years they worked together with this understanding. The call to preach has always been foremost with Ed, but the way he has carried out this call has changed several times. We started a church in a nearby town in early 1973. Ed served in several churches as interim pastor and was an associate at Thomas Road Baptist Church with Dr. Falwell. Now he has been senior pastor of Calvary Church for over fourteen years.

Although people are certainly called, a variety of ministries exist outside of preaching the Word and shepherding one's own flock. I cannot possibly address or refer to each type of ministry, and many fine books on the various kinds of ministries fill the shelves of bookstores. In most cases, however, all types of ministers and their families—not just the families of preaching/teaching clergy—must respond to situations presented to them by the people they serve.

At times, ministers find themselves in positions they did not seek. The misconceptions of those to whom ministers minister is the topic of the next chapter.

## Chapter 3

# WHAT THE PASTOR IS NOT

People's lives—even the lives of people who lead the flock—
are full of stress. We tend to look for answers and help from
those who seem more focused on God and thus more spiritual.
Their lives often appear simpler than our own.

Many times, however, people have distorted perceptions of
one another. Distorted ideas about pastors often lead to mis-
communication between lay and clergy, which in turn leads to
stress and conflict. The following are a few common misconceptions about pastors.

1. *The pastor is a substitute for God.* Some people feel that their
obligation to tend to their spiritual life is met when they show
up at a weekly service and hear a sermon. If they are not in the
habit of reading and studying the Bible, listening to a homily is
their only connection to God. People who feel the need to attend church on Christmas and Easter may do so merely to add a
religious aspect to the holidays. Since a pastor may not see many
holiday attendees for another year, their mortality and eternal
destiny weigh heavily on him, leaving him acutely aware that he
must speak the truth to them convincingly and concisely while
they are there. Still, hearing a pastor now and then is not a substitute for developing a relationship with God.

Some Christians may unintentionally look to a minister as a substitute for God and think that his every interpretation of God's Word is the sole one. Some believers get caught up in media ministries without studying the Word of God themselves. They take everything their favorite television preacher says literally. Conversations with other believers turn into "he said, she said" matches, implying that if So-and-So said it on the radio, that's the same as God speaking. Hearing and believing everything a minister says is not equivalent to learning about God through studying His Word. In fact, the Bible gives us an illustration. When Paul and Silas proclaimed to the Bereans that Jesus was Christ, "the Bereans . . . examined the Scriptures every day to see if what Paul said was true" (Acts 17:11).

Believers today should do no less. Because information from many denominations, religions, and cults is everywhere, the task of sorting truth from heresy is not easy. Nonetheless, it is our responsibility. Scripture cautions us to recognize deceivers and instructs us what to do about them (Rom. 16:17–18; Jude 7–10). The best way to avoid being deceived by impostors is to know the Scriptures (2 Tim. 3:12–17). A pastor cannot do that for anyone, and those who attend church should not expect that their pastor can somehow impart all knowledge of Scripture to them. The Holy Spirit has been sent by the Father to teach us, as Christians, about things Jesus said when He lived on earth (John 14:26). We have to do the work, however, and study our Bibles regularly.

2. *The pastor is more spiritual than everyone else.* Among early American settlers, Puritan clergy were seen as almost otherworldly. They were viewed as holy men who either did not have to deal with the temptations laypeople faced, or had conquered them. Habits of dress and general demeanor kept clergy distinct, separate, and somewhat aloof from others, and this aided in propagating the impression that they were not like "ordinary" people. All this placed a tremendous amount of pressure on the pastor and his family, not only for them to live above

reproach but also to live up to unrealistic expectations. The pastor and spouse were assumed to be more spiritual than everyone else instead of being viewed as committed servants—albeit called to ministry—on the same journey as other believers.

Today, with the rise in "seeker sensitive" churches using nontraditional methods to attract and hold members, people from secular lifestyles who become Christians are generally unaware of these once-held expectations of pastors. Some expectations, however, still exist in religious circles, especially in long-established churches. One pastor's wife wrote, "Although I have always realized my humanness and struggle with sin, I've also been aware that many in our congregations don't view us this way, and think that we as ministry leaders are somehow exempt from these struggles, having it 'all under control.'"[1]

Of course pastors must strive for God's standard: "Be holy, because I am holy" (Lev. 11:44–45; 1 Peter 1:13–16). Yet, I've talked to hundreds of people over several decades, and very often in conversation I hear a surprised gasp from church members when I refer to everyday things my husband—their pastor—has said or done. Laypeople's spiritualized images of their ministers make them seem like unreal, abnormal, and odd beings who do not behave the way other humans behave. Nothing could be further from the truth.

3. *The pastor should be placed on a pedestal.* At first glance this may appear to be the same mistake as thinking a pastor is necessarily more "holy and spiritual." But there is a difference. True, in our culture, clergy on a church pedestal are held in high esteem. The pedestal, however, is usually placed on sand instead of rock. People consider a pastor "great" if the church is "great" (that is, growing and well known). But when, for whatever reason, outward signs of church growth disappear, their tide of emotions can shift, just like those of sports fans. The pedestal and the pastor fall.

While there will always be a few who view the pastor as an

awesome figurehead above everyone else, generally in American culture the pastor is no longer set on a pedestal, to be automatically heeded and emulated. Today, the focus of religious consumers has changed "from an outward responsibility to an inward preoccupation."[2] Self-actualization—spiritualized as realizing one's giftedness—is often seen as more important than a simple obedience to God's Word. Many people within the church—no matter how faithful and hardworking the pastor is—look only to themselves, questioning if their needs are being met and seeking what will make them "feel comfortable." With that mind-set, a pastor's standing isn't a consideration.

In all fairness, the distorted perception many people have of pastors has been created, in part, by those of us in ministerial circles. Sometimes we trivialize our own calling by honoring those who build the biggest churches, hold the largest crusades, baptize the most people, record the most conversions, or have the most on the roll. Success and progress within a church, however, is not always measured in weekly statistics. It is unfortunate that we ignore the vast majority of pastors—those who faithfully and conscientiously toil in tiny congregations. Nor does our culture honor older and wiser leaders as it should—by deferring to and listening to them. (This will be addressed later). Instead, we honor people we like and criticize or ignore our Christian brothers and sisters who practice in ways that do not bring them recognition or accolades. In doing so, we have created a rift among pastoral brethren, angering some who "live in the shadows of megachurches."

It is not likely that the biblical directive to "hold them [ministers] in highest regard" refers to the distribution of honorary doctorates, preferred parking, clergy discounts, or to addressing clergy by their proper titles. This performance-based mind-set within religious enclaves does not necessarily come from our culture. It comes from a misinterpretation of one's position in Christ. The reality of that position was made clear to Ed and me one Sunday evening, early in our days at Calvary Church. We were invited to the home of some senior, long-time members of the church, along with several other couples about their same age. Songwriter John W. Peterson, who had been music minister in our church years before, and his wife were honored guests. We listened as the group discussed former pastors—who stayed how long, who came back, whose picture was not on the wall in the foyer and why not. A hilarious argument ensued. We realized that no matter how long a pastor and his family stayed in a church, we would all be in a long line of ministers and their spouses. And until the Lord's Second Coming, others would follow. We return to that perspective fairly often.

4. *The pastor is the answer man.* Because the pastor is knowledgeable in biblical matters, his name often pops into the heads of members needing answers to other unrelated matters. Ed and I have fielded questions from members regarding the phone numbers of other church or staff members, a wrecker service, the times of church services, and who can give rides to church. And for weightier matters—struggles with sexual orientation and unresolved family relationships—the pastor may seem like a therapeutic answer person. Sometimes, though, answers are not to people's liking. A biblical answer is not necessarily what everyone wants to hear. If members feel uncomfortable with the suggestions made, they may feel the pastor has failed them.

Furthermore, some types of questions do not allow for definitive answers. A member might ask, for instance, about selling a business and entering ministry full-time. A pastor cannot point to a single verse in the Bible that will tell the member what to do. He can, however, pray with members and help them sort through the steps in the decision-making process.

5. *A pastor is the parent one did not have.* When a leader's authority becomes distorted in a student's or follower's mind, transference can occur. Feelings from the past can be projected onto the minister and can wreak havoc in a church. Some church

members may look to the pastor to fulfill their needs, "putting him on a pedestal, thinking he is able to solve every problem . . . letting [their] emotions magnify those thoughts disproportionately."[3] Many pastors' spouses have indicated to me that transference of this sort is a major cause of stress in their homes. When members project their unmet needs onto clergy of the opposite sex, marriages may be at stake unless the problem is handled properly.

The most common example of transference is a woman who turns all of her attention to her pastor, often because she did not have a loving father. She may openly express her love to her pastor and/or stalk him. Another example is an individual whose family of origin has provided no support. He may cling to his pastor and constantly demand time and attention, waiting to talk after every sermon or calling often without regard to the time. While all people should get the love and attention they seek, the pastor may be hindered from helping this kind of person mature spiritually because he is constantly being emotionally drained. People who practice transference rarely accept the suggestion that they should get involved in other people's lives—they are simply too focused on their own unmet needs. For them, the role of the pastor is that of parent.

If all of the stereotypes and misconceptions described above concerned pastors only, that would be enough to cause distress. But many ministers have spouses and are parents. The lives of family members cannot be totally removed from the problems that perplex ministers. Spouses and families come under stress, and their distress affects the minister. Sometimes a cycle of conflict and unrest is perpetuated and this can distract the minister and affect his ability to serve the church.

Yet it is important for this kind of problem to be put into perspective. In an article by Dr. Gloria Halverson about coping with stress, Dr. Robert Elliot is quoted as saying, "(1) Don't sweat the small stuff, and (2) It's all small stuff."[4] While a minister's spouse may not always consider misconceptions about the minister small stuff, Dr. Halverson points out, "The things we are in a lather about today will not seem important in a week or a month—not to mention the lack of the eternal importance. Instead, we need to face life realistically. We need to exercise more grace and make fewer demands for perfection on ourselves and others."[5]

Those matters that get us "in a lather" often are truly small stuff. Not only are they small, but some may consist, not of misconceptions but of nothing more than gossip. Gossip is, according to the Bible, a sin (2 Cor. 12:20–21) and often begins as speculation. Rumors fly with particular speed if the information is intimate or puts down the subject and puffs up the talker. That's how some of the "small stuff" gets bigger, which is the next subject to be addressed.

*Chapter 4*

# THE LESS-THAN-PRIVATE
# LIVES OF PASTORS AND
# THEIR FAMILIES

Ann and Claudia had worked together in the nursery for eigh-
teen years. They had seen three pastors come and go during that
time, and they knew plenty about what really went on in the
parsonage. Between the two of them, the church membership
was well informed of the type and quality of every piece of clothing the "PKs" (pastor's kids) wore. They did not like the way
Mrs. Walder, the pastor's wife, disciplined her children, and they
openly told her that she was not a good mother. By the time
Mrs. Walder was aware of the displeasure of these women, she
found that she and her husband were on their way out. This
situation was not something that the husband could "fix" by
standing up for his wife; everything he had done for six years
had been undermined. Even though the Walders believed that
there had been a clear understanding with the church board of
their family's needs and priorities, nothing they did pleased the
people. The pastor's leadership was nonexistent. As a couple,
they had entered ministry with joyful anticipation. Now they

seriously questioned whether they had been called to the ministry at all. Their private life was fully entangled with their public ministry, and they could see no way to resolve either except to leave the church, and possibly ministry altogether.

This true story, told with the names changed, illustrates only one of a number of reasons why a pastor's public and private life is at the crux of any book or discussion about supporting and encouraging one's pastor. It is nearly impossible to write about any aspect of ministry without including its effects on the minister's family. Parts of this book may have different titles, but each category impacts or is an outgrowth of the minister's family's involvement. Decisions about a child's private, public, or home schooling are considered a lay family's private business, but they become matters of public discussion when a ministry family is involved.

Further, the stresses of our fast-paced society, which complicate laypeople's lives, also weigh heavily on the lives of ministry families. But the pastor's spouse and children have the added pressure of having to share a husband or a parent with others. The pastor's schedule becomes a never-ending balancing act—a heroic effort to give time to his family and still be available at all times for everyone else.

All public figures are likely to have their lives scrutinized, but a pastor's life is intricately and uniquely involved with those to whom he ministers, because they expect and hope that he will demonstrate the type of character they need from a leader. Church members often find themselves referring to the pastor's family in their conversations at home when they sort through their own decisions. Without even realizing it, church members often hold the ministry family up as an example of how families should be. Ed and I did the same thing to our senior pastor when our children were young. A discussion might end something like this: "If Jerry Falwell never missed one of his children's birthday parties even though he could have accepted

invitations to preach on those dates, then we shouldn't schedule ourselves away on our children's important days either."
Because we could see that Jerry and Macel put their children
first above other earthly relationships, we decided that we
should do no less. Perhaps we should not have used the example of another family to help us make this kind of decision. Certainly, it is scary to think that now at least some of
the people in our congregation look at our family and do the
same thing.

A young mother told me she had been urging her daughter
to join a junior high ministry team at church, but the girl did not
want to because she did not have any close friends on any of the
teams. She was, however, involved in two sports and another
extracurricular activity in school. The daughter's attitude about
life was generally good, and she enjoyed going to church. The
mom said to me, "You've been through it. How did you handle
your children's involvement with church activities?"

I realized that decisions we had made and issues we had sorted
through privately with our children were now, in essence, becoming part of our public ministry. My response seemed to surprise
her: "Don't force the issue. Several of our children were so excited
about all of the ministry opportunities in middle school that by the
time they reached tenth grade, they had gone everywhere and done
everything. One chose not to do anything but go to church the last
few years of school, and another waited until her senior year to get
involved again. Opportunities will be there for your daughter when
she is ready to participate, and she will love them if she is the one
who makes the choice. It won't be real ministry if she joins a team
because you want her to."

It is true that the pastor of a church is a public figure. But, unlike
public figures in the political arena, who usually spend years preparing themselves emotionally and mentally as they work their way to
top positions, a pastor simply answers God's call and spends a few
years in formal education in preparation for a lifetime of ministry.

Another difference between politicians and pastors lies in public perception. Regarding moral purity, corruption among politicians is not uncommon. Voters rarely take it into account when they are at the polls. Pastors' lives, however, are under great scrutiny by those who hear them teach the Bible. Because they are teaching Truth, it is essential that the lives of pastors be above reproach, that they live what they preach. If they fail morally, they may lose both their families and ministries. Fallen politicians may lose their families, but they seldom lose their positions. They sometimes have to resign if they have been accused of breaking a law, but adultery is not a crime in our legal system.

Moreover, a moral failure in the life of a politician does not have the same ripple effect as that of someone in ministry. The ministry family is not just tagging along for the ride, and certainly not for the perks (although there are distinct advantages that will be addressed later). The spouse and children are woven into the fabric of ministry life whether they like it or not.

Some distinctly do not like it. They may be struggling with submission to God's will for their lives or with their own identity and the complications of other unresolved matters. In such cases, ministry couples sometimes end up dissolving their marriage. In doing so they devastate more people than their own family. It is very difficult for church members when their role models have broken their vows. Members of the congregation may drive by the parsonage for years, wondering if any of the couples who occupied it had loving, intimate relationships— relationships at all worth emulating.

"The pastoral ministry is unique in that no other professional family lives and works within a larger family—the congregation."[1] Other professionals do not face the same kind of expectations as do the minister and his family. The whole ministry family is under the watchful eye of the church members, some of whom do not allow for any variables; only perfection will do. Many ministry wives talk about "living in a fishbowl," where they have no privacy. But we in the ministry must keep in mind what is truly important. Regarding life in the limelight,

> Quality people see to it that Jesus is kept as the center-piece of their service for Christ. They know ministry is always fouled or frustrated when anyone usurps the Lord's place, even in small ways. This leads to a challenging question: Could it be that some who complain about the fishbowl existence of ministry secretly enjoy being in the limelight? . . . [Living] a Christ-quality life is a delightful way to live that takes us above and beyond any imposed or implied directives from others.[2]

The following are some of the areas of ministry life that are under the microscope.

## Children

A pastor was deeply hurt by certain people in his congregation. He needed time to express his frustration at home during the hardest days, so his wife told their young children to play quietly in their rooms when Daddy came home. "He's sad because some people are saying things that hurt his feelings," the mother told the oldest child, a preschooler. After about thirty minutes, the girl emerged from her room. "I'm sorry you got an owie, Daddy. Here's a big kiss to make it all better."

Ministry couples must decide how much information to give their children about issues and people in the church. In the incident mentioned above, the mother knew the whole picture but did not want to explain it fully to her children. She simply wanted them to know that their father was hurting, that not all people loved everything Daddy was doing. Children sometimes overhear parts of conversations not meant for their ears. Their parents must give them only enough information to settle any unrest in their hearts. At times they may wish to involve the whole family in prayer. Confidential matters, especially those of immorality, must not be divulged. Children need to learn that everyone else's business is not necessarily theirs. It is difficult to decide how much to tell a pastor's children about disagreements people have with their father or mother. Some children are devastated when they see their dad or mom openly criticized or refuted in congregational meetings. The children learn a lot about God's character, as well as their parents' character, when they see how their parents react to these situations. Children should learn that people, including their parents, are not perfect, but that God is trustworthy, in control, and can change people's hearts.[3]

No matter how hard a ministry couple tries to bring their children up normally, eventually the children learn that people in the church are watching them in a way that they do not watch other children. After all, there are biblical principles for ministry leaders to follow: "He must manage his own family well and see that his children obey him with proper respect" (1 Tim. 3:4); a minister must be "a man whose children believe and are not open to the charge of being wild and disobedient" (Titus 1:6). Without a well-managed family and household, a leader does not have an "excellent standing" (1 Tim. 3:12–13). When a person feels called to be an "overseer" or "deacon," or whatever label one wants to put on a ministry position, he places the whole family in the spotlight. Some people think that means the pastor's children should be on a tether, never allowed to make decisions for themselves or to enjoy lives apart from the church. These people do not like to see their pastors taken away from church activities to watch their own children participate in outside activities.

When our children reached the age for high school activities, Ed and I cut back on entertaining church members. We enjoyed having people in our home, but we wanted to go to high school games or events which were of interest to, if not participated in, by our own children. We often found ourselves explaining that we did not want our children to "hate us for being too involved with the church to be involved in their lives." One of our children tried to hold that statement over our heads. The child wanted to do something that would have taken us away from a church commitment we had already made. We must always struggle for balance. The boundaries of involvement in ministry and private lives have had to be redefined periodically, and we do not expect all church members to understand or agree with every decision we make about our children.

Sometimes children of ministers get a bad reputation because they deserve it. But sometimes responsible children of ministers are unfairly given the cold shoulder. Josh, for instance, was not given an interview for an advertised job at the church his father pastored. He was bluntly told the reason—in times past, the child of a pastor had not been a satisfactory worker. There was no attempt to check the references from Josh's former employers. In a secular arena, the family might have hollered "Discrimination!" But in Josh's case, the family felt it was best not to say anything and to avoid an unpleasant scene. Josh took the incident in stride, feeling that it was better not to be employed by someone with that attitude. Openly discussing these matters at home helps the ministry family maintain a healthy perspective, allowing them to do what is right as believers, rather than trying to live up to other people's expectations.

Ministry children are branded as "PKs," which sets them apart from others, usually with snide comments about their behavior or—even more often—dress. There is probably no more obvious arena for misunderstanding the pastor's children than in what they wear. A music minister once said to Kent, our teenage son, whose T-shirt hung over his sloppy jeans and whose hair hung down to his shoulders, "I see that you have grasped the biblical principle that man looks on the outward appearance, but God looks on the heart."

When Kent was in sixth grade, a mom told me that she thought our son was a poor example for her son, because ours did not wear a suit and tie on Sundays. My husband, who heard her challenge, responded kindly, "I would rather see a child who is willing to come to church wear *any* kind of clothing than to hate to come when forced to dress a certain way. Church won't be beneficial for him if he hates to come."

Sometimes Kent would come to church late and walk up to the front to sit by me after I had played the piano. Sure, I used to wish he looked more preppy, or at least a little more the way people expected him to look. In submission to my husband's beliefs, however, I thanked the Lord that my son took a shower every day, wore clean clothes, was respectful of house rules, was dependable in his job, and didn't mind being seen with us. Kent is in full-time ministry now, married to a godly, sweet wife. He still does not conform to the image some people think he should have. But he shows a willingness to conform to the image of God's Son. No parent could wish for anything better.

Feeling the need to live up to a public image of the perfect ministry family, the pastor and spouse may encounter years of stress if a child's image does not meet everyone's approval. When children become old enough to make their own decisions about righteous or sinful behavior, many parent/pastors find themselves in board meetings ready to resign from ministry either out of shame or a broken heart. They may even find themselves forced out by the church. This matter will be discussed further in the chapter on talking face-to-face with the pastor.

Overall, most ministry parents probably want their children to do right for the right reasons. But they sometimes convey to their children that image is more important than it should be. Children, at times, as Cameron Lee and Jack Balswick write, feel that the disapproval of members of the congregation "influences, if not overrides, the parents' opinion. At the very least, on an issue where a minister and spouse may be neutral regarding their children's behavior [such as skipping church], pressure from the congregation may tip the scales."[4] The same authors use the term *triangling* to describe what occurs when members or staff engage a pastor and/or his spouse in a conflict of opinion over the pastor's children. It takes courage for parents to face and deal with these issues in a way that will not spiritually alienate their children. It might not be until the children are grown up and can openly express their feelings or write their own books that their parents will finally realize the extreme pressure they were under—pressure to live exemplary lives long before they had reached spiritual maturity.

Another dilemma for ministry parents occurs when their children get married. It is almost impossible to determine which church members are intimate friends and which are only close acquaintances. If the parents fail to include people who are sincerely interested in the marrying child, they might cause disappointment or offense. Because of financial constraints and the size of the church, the pastor's family may be unable to invite all those they would like to the wedding and reception. People tell ministry parents, not entirely in jest, to allow themselves plenty of time to save up for a wedding. That, too, may pose problems that cannot be kept altogether private. Not every pastor and spouse have opportunities to earn extra money or to take time away from their commitment and calling to moonlight. Some church boards place restrictions on their pastors keeping money earned from outside sources. And that brings us to the next item for scrutiny.

# Salary

Board member to pastoral prospect: "We want a monthly statement of your expenditures."

Pastoral prospect: "Really? Can I expect the same from you?"

Board member: "No. We pay your salary, so we have a right

to know where every dime goes—phone calls, credit card debts, home improvements, vacations, and so forth."

Believe it or not, the man took the job! Because the pastor's salary is open knowledge for the congregation, many church members feel that they should have input regarding the way the money is spent. True, the pastor should exemplify good stewardship and accountability to the board, practicing restraint and avoiding poor spending habits and debt. However, the fine line between public and private is crossed when church members (and even other ministry personnel) feel free to drop hints about how their pastor should spend his money. While restraint is a good thing, it can cause stress when ministry couples base too many decisions on "how it might look," or "what will people think?"

But wait. It gets even more complex. *How it might look* has its pluses as well as its minuses. On the minus side, it kept us from buying a house with a swimming pool when we first moved into this community. The property was priced well below what one might expect and was an exceptional value. But we passed it up, feeling it might appear too extravagant and that the luxury of a swimming pool would raise more than a few eyebrows. On the plus side, when our concern about "how it might look" made us think twice, we realized that we could not afford the extra expense for pool maintenance. I also feared that a toddler might wander into it and drown. That is not to say that pastors should not ever have a swimming pool, but it was not the prudent thing for us at that time.

Ed and I, along with many other people in ministry, appreciate that the minister's salary comes from gifts that people make to the work of God. We feel a responsibility to make wise decisions about its use. At times, however, privacy in regard to spending seems unattainable—which can be frustrating. That is why people in ministry need to be reminded by their peers that their integrity may be at stake when they discuss salary issues.

One pastor's wife says, "Few professions receive the tax breaks enjoyed by ministers. Whenever we humbly acknowledge our salary is 'x-amount' and neglect to explain that is x plus our housing, insurance, car, and professional designations, we lack integrity."[5] Specific benefits such as health insurance, life insurance, or retirement programs vary in churches. Ministry families, as well as all staff, should be grateful if their church provides benefits for family members as well as employees. Coverage for family members is an added blessing, especially when one realizes that the gifts of God's people make it possible. Not all laypeople are so fortunate in their jobs.

A biblical principle that keeps money management in perspective is 1 Timothy 3:7: "He [the overseer] must also have a good reputation with outsiders, so that he will not fall into disgrace and into the devil's trap." This reputation includes much more than financial dealings in the community. But a called one who is spiritually mature and humble (v. 6) will strive to manage the money he earns through a ministry in a way that pleases God. Sadly, some ministers get heavily into debt when there is no accountability or advisory procedure provided through the board of the church. We have enjoyed the benefit of knowing people of good reputation who have been able to advise us in personal financial matters as well as inform us of culturally sensitive matters within our community. This was true in our first church and continues today.

# Housing

Jane heard a knock on their parsonage door, but she could not dress quickly enough to answer it.

"Hello," a voice called.

"I can't come to the door," Jane replied from the bathtub.

"It's OK. I just want to show Aunt Millie the parsonage."

Jane heard voices and footsteps through the house, and finally the front door clicked shut. That was the last time they left the door unlocked.

When a pastor's family lives in a parsonage or manse (a home owned by the church), they may feel that they have less privacy than ministry families who are responsible for their own housing. They may not be as free to make personal choices in home decorating. Indeed, many members of congregations have let a pastor's wife know of their displeasure when she wanted to change the carpet or wallpaper in a house owned by the church. Freedom to redecorate the parsonage is a matter that should be clarified with the church board, but even so, many a paint job has resulted in division within the church.

Some pastors and their spouses see advantages to living in church-owned homes: they need only one car, they have no need to house-hunt, and they can stay home until the last minute before leaving for church. Living in a parsonage, however, creates challenges at retirement or in cases of forced termination.

If pastors own their own homes, their sizes and locations create other issues related to salary and image (mentioned in the above section). Ministers may fear misunderstandings if their home is in a neighborhood considered, on the one hand, too expensive, or on the other, beneath that of many of the church members. The same is true regarding the make and model of the pastor's car. Some of our ministerial friends drive the finest cars available, and their church community would not think of having it any other way. Many ministry families opt for an affordable, dependable, and not-too-noticeably luxurious kind of car.

Because our American culture is so different from biblical times, and because there are no specific Scriptures that address this particular problem, pastors and church members can only gain some hints from the past about appropriate housing for ministers. In the early church, people met in homes. We do not know how big those groups were, so the size of the home probably does not matter. It is important, however, that people who came into the home of mature believers were welcomed in love by Christian brothers and sisters. The atmosphere for learning about God and growing in grace came from the husband's calling and standing among believers. But the tone in the home was set by the wife, who was to be "temperate, self-controlled, respectable, hospitable, able to teach, not given to drunkenness, not violent but gentle, not quarrelsome, not a lover of money" (1 Tim. 3:2–3).

It may seem impossible for any couple in ministry to live up to this demanding textbook example. Consider the position of a young couple just starting out in their ministry experience. Note, though, that these instructions were given to Timothy by Paul, the older disciple teaching the younger. Paul also tells Timothy to train himself to be godly (4:7); "don't let anyone look down on you because you are young" (v. 12); and to be "diligent . . . so that everyone may see your progress" (v. 15). Even though Timothy had been mentored by Paul over a period of time and had become trustworthy and responsible as a church leader, he was still growing. We, too, as ministry personnel are still growing even if we, like Timothy (2 Tim. 1:5), come from several generations of committed believers.

*Chapter 5*

# HELP FOR THE JOURNEY

"People can be so cruel." As a young pastor's wife, I often heard this phrase from older women whose husbands had been in ministry for years. They would not talk about what they meant, but I sensed that they had been deeply wounded by people in the churches they had served. I determined not to let the harsh or cruel side of people hurt me. I thought that my attitude was positive enough to carry me above any ugly words—words that would probably be based on situations existing before Ed and I had arrived on the scene. But I learned that I was not immune to cutting remarks.

A chiropractor once told me that he treats more pastors' wives than any other segment of society. Most people, he said, underestimate the effects of people-induced stress on the body. In many cases, this stress can be worked out in the yard, in the gym, or by heavy-duty cleaning. But a pastor's wife must cope with an element that paid staff do not experience. She must internalize the problems of troubled members and, at the same time—because of confidentiality—never express concerns about the church the way other members can. All this can weigh heavily on her spirit, taking a physical toll. A pastor's wife is well advised to recognize this possibility and get help if necessary. Sometimes her concerns may be overexaggerated or unfounded, but at other times her fears may be entirely realistic.

One young wife, for example, was afraid for her pastor husband. The most prominent bootlegger in the mountains was angry that his wife had become a Christian. He told the pastor, "I'm coming into town to shoot you!" Not surprisingly, the pastor found himself wondering if he'd made the right career choice. But he told the man he would be waiting on the steps of the church. The man never showed up.

That young pastor was my husband, and for a period of time after that I was concerned for his life, as I have been a number of times over the years. Once, we were awakened during the night by a phone call. The man on the other end of the line did not identify himself or ask to whom he was speaking. All he did was scream over the phone that Ed had been having sex with his wife and he was coming to shoot him. I heard Ed reply, "I think you have the wrong number." Fortunately, the man didn't call back or come to the house.

No one can fully estimate the toll that ministry takes on the lives of ministers and their families—although, as I must often reiterate, there is much joy on the journey as well. As a result of the intense personal needs and stresses (which I've come to call "stressures") on people in ministry, dozens of support ministries have arisen all over the world to help pastors and their families. *Caregiver* is a term for those who have dedicated their lives to helping ministers and their families meet the challenges of ministry life. Pastors cannot always look for help within their own church, and the potential for division within a denomination is a concern if pastors open their problems to peers. Thus, in order to keep matters private, pastors will often turn to helpers outside their circle of influence.

While some denominations do provide counseling, retreats, financial advice, and legal aid for their personnel, there are still thousands of ministers who are not connected to any fellowship or denomination, who have heartfelt needs, but do not know where to turn.

Nondenominational ministries to pastors exist in most states. They sometimes consist of newsletters or other forms of peer encouragement, marriage enrichment, renewal retreats, and treatment centers. Many services are offered free, and others charge low or graduated fees. Although a few of the ministries have become nationally known, I have found that about half of the ministry wives I know are not aware of caregiving ministries outside their own circles. It is very common for people in ministry to be so engrossed in their particular religious world that they are oblivious of the many resources that have become available in the last ten to fifteen years. It is only when pastors and/or their wives and families reach a crisis point—"a code blue"—that they discover help is not far away. It is a sad fact that by then their situation may be headline news, and their departure from ministry inevitable.

Knowledge of these caregivers is of interest to laypeople as well as to career ministers. Sometimes laypeople are close to their ministers and sense that the pastor, spouse, or family needs help from outside the church. They can suggest caregivers or provide the financial resources to take advantage of them. Often laypeople have been burdened and felt called by the Lord to start caregiving ministries, and even to network among themselves so that the caregivers do not become burned out while ministering to ministers. Mature, godly, sensitive laypeople can sometimes see that their ministers are hurting, that they are battered at times by their peers or by church members. A church board member, for instance, may be aware of difficult situations the pastor must handle and sense help is needed. Or perhaps a church member may see a clergy family in the community who is in crisis and offer a secluded vacation house to the weary couple. In each case, Christian brothers and sisters minister to one another, pointing one another to the Savior, who is the true

Caregiver. Each recognizes that a pastor is a human being with needs, not a superhuman who is less vulnerable than everyone else.

The most comprehensive current information is available on the Internet at www.pastorsnet.org, a site that details a two-pronged ministry—one for laypeople and another for ministry personnel. EQUIP (Encouraging Qualities Undeveloped in People) for laypeople was founded by John Maxwell, a former pastor, whose mission is now to develop leaders in all areas of life. As a senior pastor, he inspired and trained laypeople to pray for their pastors. (The importance of prayer ministry to and for pastors will be discussed in the next chapter.) Dennis Worden now directs the prayer ministry, called Partners in Prayer, as well as the other prong for ministry personnel, CareGiver Ministries, which links pastors and their families with caregivers by providing a directory. The directory is constantly being expanded and updated. The toll-free number for it is 1-888-993-7847.

The healthy cycle works this way: ministers teach the Word and learners grow in grace, telling the Good News to unbelievers. Followers of Jesus learn that every believer is called to "do good to all people, especially those who belong to the family of believers" (Gal. 6:10). By doing good to all believers (including one's pastor) a follower's personal ministry expands, from telling people about Christ and helping them become mature Christians, to ministering to their own ministers. That is the way a loving Christian brotherhood should work.

Sometimes it takes the forthright zeal of a committed layperson to "get in the face" of a severely depressed minister and say, "It is obvious to me that you are deeply troubled. Is anything in your life hindering you or weighing you down?" If the time is right, and the other person seems to be receptive, he may be able to suggest that they read Hebrews 12:1–3 together and spend time talking about the importance of fixing our eyes on Jesus. Done in a loving and nonjudgmental way, accompanied by prolonged prayer and follow-up that may include suggestions for a physical checkup and Christian professional counseling, the layperson can have a profound impact on the life of a minister.

While many ministers and their families have been aided by support ministries like the ones mentioned above, in some instances no amount of loving, caring, confronting, counseling, or accountability will keep a person in ministry from falling, from burnout, or even from committing suicide. When a minister resigns in disgrace or dies by his own hand, the effects are devastating and long lasting. The private pain and suffering of the minister is passed on to the public, or at the very least to his congregation and others whose lives have been touched by that minister. Specialized ministries have been developed to try to reach the hearts of people who have "given up on God" or on organized religion as a result of being involved in or witnessing a spiritual crisis.

Ministry is more than sharing the gospel; it is helping people in the family of God as they travel the long and sometimes painful path to spiritual maturity. Stuart Briscoe once said, if even Peter could end his letter to Christians by telling them to grow in grace (2 Peter 3:18), then "there is always room for growth." Even the oldest and most faithful saints in ministry can experience growth. "Ministry by definition is a partnership with God. We are never alone in our efforts for God and for His people."[1] When ministers feel alone, they need support and encouragement from God. They may beg Him to send His help. Caregivers, whether formally organized or not, are heaven sent. They help ministers see that sometimes even God's called servants have to step away from their routines for personal growth, refreshment, renewal, and healing.

A visiting minister told our church that Adoniram Judson was the first American to take the gospel to Burma (Miranmar), and believers there today trace their spiritual heritage to him. Any modern missionary would be delighted to have even a fraction of the influence he had on Christianity. Yet Judson did not see a single convert for seven years, he buried two wives and several children, and then he suffered a nervous breakdown. Judson's story serves as an example for today's missionaries in far-flung places, as well as for the congregations that sponsor them. Although an abundance of caregiving ministries exist in America, they are not all easily accessible to everyone in ministry, and many ministry personnel cannot admit their need for care until they are completely broken and out of the ministry.

One biblical example of a caregiver to a traveling missionary is Epaphroditus (Phil. 2:15–30; 4:18). Paul describes him as a fellow worker, a fellow soldier, and a messenger. Epaphroditus was actually involved in ministry. He carried gifts to Paul from the church at Philippi and took care of Paul's needs much the same as short-term missionaries today carry supplies and encourage ministers or missionaries in foreign countries. Epaphroditus risked his health and life for the cause of Christ. He may have traveled seven hundred miles, no easy feat in those days. Paul's important instruction to the church was that they should honor people like Epaphroditus. His works alone would inspire anyone who has a desire to serve the Lord. When we read the way Paul describes the life of his friend, we realize how important ministry supporters are to ministers. They are a source of joy for a saddened heart. Biblical precedence exists, then, for honoring caregivers. And even they need to be encouraged.

Nobody wants to be ministered to by people who, through too much stress, have come to feel sorry for themselves. That is an important reason why caregivers exist, and why pastors and their families should not hesitate to seek their services. Above all, however, ministry families can look to biblical principles for a good perspective on the call and the purpose of ministry work: "Therefore, my dear brothers, stand firm. Let nothing move you. Always give yourselves fully to the work of the Lord, because you know that your labor in the Lord is not in vain" (1 Cor.

15:58). Not in vain. What a comfort, knowing that our greatest resource for support is God. And He uplifts in ways not at first obvious.

Early in Ed's ministry, Frank and Alicia, who were on the verge of divorce, started coming to our new church. They were already separated when they made an appointment to see Ed. He was a newlywed himself and had never done any marriage counseling. He was so scared that he stayed up late the night before to read a book on it.

For several hours Ed listened to Frank and Alicia yell at each other and throw accusations back and forth. When he had had enough, Ed stopped them and said that they needed to forget the past and forgive each other. They all got down on their knees, and the couple did exactly that! They never had any further counseling. The Spirit and the Word of God changed their hearts and lives.

Ed no longer practices marriage counseling and recognizes that people's lives are often too complicated for the simple directive that cured Frank and Alicia's marital problem. It is a monument to God that His mercy and grace was more than sufficient to make up for Ed's inexperience at that moment. Over twenty years later, however, Frank called Ed to thank him for his ministry during that critical time in their lives.

"Your labor in the Lord is not in vain." What a hope that someday we—ministers and all who in myriad ways labor for Christ—will realize that many of the hard times we endured had a bright side, that even when we were unaware lives were touched and changed by the Word.

*Section 2*

# SUPPORTING YOUR PASTOR

*Chapter 6*

# R-E-S-P-E-C-T

Having looked at what the pastor does and how the call to ministry plays a part in the family life of a pastor, we now turn to the Bible to see what it has to say about the way the lives of ministry people and laypeople interweave.

Is there a model in Scripture that church members can use as a guideline when they want to communicate support to their minister? The Bible says we have "everything we need for life and godliness through our knowledge of him who called us by his own glory and goodness" (2 Peter 1:3). We don't need to look further than God's Word.

But what is written in Scripture about the subject can easily be missed. After all, we are not discussing major doctrines. Instructions may only appear in the opening or conclusion of epistles, or in subtleties gleaned from stories throughout the Bible. Until I began to study the Word with this subject in mind, I thought that there were very few verses on it. Much more is implied in Scripture, however, and can be applied to the way Christians treat each other. There are a number of specific comments that will be looked at throughout this book. Wherever a biblical reference is suggested, it would benefit the reader to look up the passage and read the paragraphs preceding and following the verse in order to gain a broader context.

Perhaps one of the clearest instructions with regard to supporting spiritual leaders is in Paul's letter to the church in Thessalonica—a church that was founded during his second missionary journey (Acts 17:1–10). He tells the family of God to "respect those who work hard among you, who are over you in the Lord and who admonish you. Hold them in the highest regard in love because of their work. Live in peace with each other" (1 Thess. 5:12–13).

Before looking at individual words in this passage from Thessalonians, we should first note the setting and the recipients of this letter from Paul. The environment of this newly formed church in Thessalonica was hostile to Christianity. The new believers needed Paul's words of exhortation, comfort, and hope to spur them to live pure lives in preparation for Christ's return. The message applies to us as well.

*"Respect those who work hard among you . . ."* Webster's Dictionary defines *respect* as admiration, consideration, deference. People with secularized values may not understand the true meaning of the word. Individuals in our society have become increasingly hostile to authority. Millions of children grow up without anyone worthy of respect to look up to. They are taught by society that their own rights are what matter most and that consideration of others is of low priority.

Our country has in many ways lost its sense of respect and reverence for God, not only in churches but also in the way we live out our lives. We want to seek comfort and demand our rights. If we respect neither God nor our spiritual leaders, we are not likely to respect ourselves.

But do church members have godly examples to follow? Ed went to a major car race in the South. Over the public-address system, a Baptist minister prayed for God to bless the drivers and the sponsors. In case you are unfamiliar with car races, many of the sponsors are beer and tobacco companies. Do we in the Christian community really want to invoke God's blessings on companies whose sole purpose is to make money by selling products that ruin health and families? If I attended that pastor's church and I were struggling with an addiction to nicotine or alcohol, would I be able to respect him if he blessed what for me is a curse in my life?

The people in the Thessalonian church saw their ministers working hard among them. We admire someone who puts on work clothes, someone who is unafraid of dirt and sweat, and who accomplishes as much as possible. That person earns our respect. Most pastors work more than a forty-hour week. In fact, many fail to take time away from work for family and for personal Sabbath. Although a pastor earns the respect of the church people more by loving them and preaching the Word than he does by working many hours, nonetheless, dealing with the never-ending needs of people requires hard work. The congregation who, with joy, follows the leadership of its pastor, and who best demonstrates spiritual growth, sees its pastor as a servant leader (slave to God) rather than as someone who wants his edicts obeyed.

*"Who are over you in the Lord . . ."* The ministers in Thessalonica who deserved respect were "over" the brothers, not in the sense of "lording over" them or putting on an air of authority. Rather, those leaders were mature believers, guiding and directing the affairs of the church. Dictatorship in churches produces immature followers. Pastors who lead by dictatorship or by "lording over" the congregation are an easy setup for moral failure, because no one is allowed to hold them accountable. Anyone who questions his methods or actions is branded as unspiritual or worse. As one pastor wrote to his fellow pastors, "In our pastoral office we must not lord it over the flock. An unsanctified pride of office is nowhere more repulsive than in a Christian minister. Yet, by virtue of his post and vocation, a measure of dignity invests his counsel in spiritual affairs."[1]

In the book of Matthew, Jesus' disciples were arguing over

who would sit next to Him in the kingdom. In answer, Jesus mentioned the nature of discipleship. Although the church was still in formation, He made it clear that His followers were not to "lord it over" those who were under their authority (20:28). Today, some religious leaders, like Jesus' disciples, want to sit on the platform next to their idol or have their names printed with that person's on programs or publications. Jesus taught leaders to become slaves, following His example. A mature layperson can detect intuitively whether a leader is living according to Jesus' directive or whether his actions show that he is merely eager to be seen with important people and thereby be seen as important. Even children of pastors know when their parents are trying to climb the ecclesiastical ladder rather than putting God and family first.

The Old Testament addresses the problem of "lording over." Nehemiah saw governors taking advantage of the people, stealing money, food, and wine; their "administrative assistants" were lording it over the people. Today that would translate as, "Don't fool with me, I'm church staff." Nehemiah made it clear that he did not live that way: "But out of reverence for God I did not act like that. Instead, I devoted myself to the work" (Neh. 5:15–16). When God's servants stick to their call, their fear of God keeps them from taking advantage of the people.

*"Who admonish you . . ."* In Thessalonica, church leaders were teachers in word and deed "who admonish," just as pastors are today. One thesaurus states that to admonish is to advise, caution, counsel, and warn. Thus ministers should not be new Christians. They need to have traveled down the spiritual journey long enough that they are credible when they are teaching believers the whole counsel of God—the joys of the Christian life as well as the pitfalls, dangers, and battles.

The writer of Hebrews takes this idea of credibility a step further: "Remember your leaders, who spoke the word of God to you. Consider the outcome of their way of life and imitate their faith" (13:7). Paul exhorted the Jewish Christians to "remember their spiritual fathers," because remembering their characters gave "credence to (their) message."[2] In other words, what ministers say is believable because of the way they live. The apostle Paul was so confident that the way he lived was consistent with what he taught "everywhere in every church" that he urged believers to imitate him (1 Cor. 4:16). Nothing finer can be said of pastors' characters than that they walk (live) what they talk. When pastors are like that, church members can with confidence heed the command "obey your leaders and submit to their authority. They keep watch over you as [persons] who must give an account. Obey them so that their work will be a joy, not a burden, for that would be of no advantage to you" (Heb. 13:17). Ray Stedman wrote that Paul was, in essence, saying, "These [leaders] are concerned about your souls' welfare, and although they may have to speak rather harshly at times, it's not because they want to hurt you, but to help you."[3]

Because the general trend in modern society is to refuse to recognize any claims for authority, in many churches today "the pastor is not recognized as having the moral authority to call people to make changes in their lifestyles or their giving patterns. . . . In these circumstances, what is left to the pastor is to keep everybody happy."[4] What pastor would not love to have a happy congregation? Unfortunately, even if keeping people happy were the main mission, it would be an impossibility.

*"Hold them in the highest regard . . ."* Highest regard? But the Bible says that God alone is worthy of our highest honor (Rev. 4:9–11), so what does it mean for us to hold in high regard or to give honor to his called servant? As one author says,

> We are not to drain our pastors dry for our benefit. We are not to have relationships with them just to meet our needs, of which each honest, authentic person has more than his or her "fair" share. If we truly believe that the

church is like a body, then those of us who are elbows, or kneecaps, or whatever, cannot forget to honor, pay attention to, and love those at the "head" of our local bodies [churches].[5]

First Timothy 6:1 gives us another clue as to the way to give high regard: "All who are under the yoke of slavery should consider their masters worthy of full respect, so that God's name and our teaching may not be slandered." At first glance this passage seems irrelevant both to this discussion and to modern society. Pastors are certainly not "masters" of the congregation and the congregation is not a "slave" to church leadership. Elders, deacons, and staff are only servants of God. But in the time of the apostle Paul, a slave's heart was changed when, through a church leader's teaching, he or she came to know the Lord and thereby honored God's name. That slave's new attitude was reflected in the respect shown to his or her master. Today, Christ is the Master, and what a joy it is for ministers to see believers, through their teaching, choosing to live according to God's precepts.

*"Live in peace with each other."* This is not for pastors only. Each one of us must make it happen in our own lives. It is a call to avoid gossip, troublemaking, and the stirring up of dissension (Prov. 6:19; 10:12; 15:18; Gal. 5:20; Rom. 13:13). Many believers, however, both laypeople and ministers alike, do not live in peace. Some think that the "worse" sins, such as homosexuality and divorce, should be the focus of condemnation in the church. In doing so, they do not try to rid themselves of their own "little sins"—as if God would easily overlook them.

Living in peace is not so much an action as an outcome of living in obedience to God's commands: "Love one another deeply" (1 Peter 1:22); "Be devoted to one another in brotherly love. Honor one another above yourselves," or, as the King James Version states, "in honour preferring one another" (Rom. 12:10).

What does all this preaching-gone-off-to-meddlin' have to do with supporting your pastor? Those who are not on the path to holy living cannot provide an oasis to a servant of the Lord. At the same time, the way the pastor lives should reflect a godly character worth imitating, honoring, and respecting. In the New Testament, Paul stated that the transformed Corinthian believers' lives were the same as letters of recommendation or introduction (2 Cor. 3:1–2). In what ways could you, as a church member, say that your life reflects the ministry of your pastor so well that he could use it on a ministry flyer or tract? The testimony of such a life gives pastors the confidence and the joy to continue ministry.

Let each of us, as believers, determine to live obediently to God's commands. Let us live in peace with one another. If we do so, our spiritual depth can provide the oasis a ministry person might need when the well seems dry and the journey long. That is more than just a cup of cool water—it is a spring in the desert.

*Chapter 7*

# A SPRING IN THE DESERT

Congregations can often be an important support for clergy families during joyous, tragic, and sometimes heart-wrenching times. Their sensitivity during the lowest and highest times of ministry life can potentially be the difference between a pastor's decision to leave ministry or stay in it.

When pastors sense that they are "drying up" spiritually, they can go to their own Shepherd for refreshing. But Christian brothers and sisters can help too. They can be like springs in the desert, coming to their pastor's aid or at least not hindering him from being rejuvenated. In fact, the bond of Christian brotherhood can sometimes be more comforting than that of families.

On the other hand, Christian brothers and sisters can be caustic. We could all do with some "sensitivity training" to help us see one another's perspective. Better sensitivity would help us know when our ministers needed support, and how we could best share their burdens.

Many times a congregation has surrounded Ed and me with love and ministered to us. And we know of many congregations who have offered support to ministry families who were in need of critical care for extended periods. Some pastors have not been able to preach for many months, either because of ill health or family crises. Their members have tenderly cared for them and willingly taken on the burden of finding guest ministers to fill the pulpit.

The following examples may inspire and encourage you to reach out to ministry families, as well as to any other people you may know who are in need.

One of the most difficult situations a parent can face, apart from the death of a child, is a child's incarceration. Prison Fellowship has reported that the church is not always a safe haven for the parents of prisoners. Sometimes a church does not know how to deal with uncomfortable issues such as domestic violence.[1] When these problems actually occur within the parsonage, an unprepared or spiritually immature church may respond in stunned silence. Some members may advocate dismissing the pastor at this very time when comfort and care are most needed—comfort and care, it might be added, that the pastor has willingly given to members of the congregation in similar situations.

One pastor's wife had wondered for years whether her husband had made a mistake accepting the call to the church where they were serving. For years this woman had wished to be somewhere else—anywhere else. At least her family life seemed normal. Normal, that is, until one of their children, who had never caused any grief to the family, was caught in sinful activity and received a harsh jail sentence. The congregation rallied. It displayed such love and steadfastness that it completely changed her view. Women helped in tangible ways—housecleaning, meals, and child care for the family, and letter writing to the one in prison encouraging spiritual growth and courage. Some prayed daily for the boy's safety, others for his mental state. One even prayed for the prison guards. People made a point of hugging this hurting mother every week in church. They cried with her and let her know that she was not shouldering the pain alone. In fact, at times she wanted to comfort them! The ministry couple found themselves growing closer to each other and to their church family, and they thanked God for working in all their lives. People in the congregation, in turn, knew that their pastor, because of his suffering, understood the trials they were going through. He was able to teach them what God was teaching him as a hurting father. A new ministry was formed, aimed at people outside the church who were going through a similar experience.

The pastor's wife was able to realize that "people were open to us because we weren't perfect. . . . They felt they could talk to us. The whole experience was humbling. We had to trust God completely. We had nothing to offer but God's Word and the person of Christ. It's so easy to forget [who we are] and think we're the important person and that we're the example, but we're only sinners saved by the grace of God."

This couple probably believed that they had already been trusting God completely. When their world was shattered, however, they became acutely aware of their utter helplessness and their dependence on God. The publicity they suffered, in the end, worked for good. The people in their church came to know that they were ministered to by real people who experience real struggles and pain just like they did. Until that incident, the pastor's wife had felt that she should keep her struggles to herself, "trying to create the image that [we've] got it all together and that [we] have all the answers." She was gratified to learn that the congregation would uphold them, fallible as they were.

Other ministry couples are not so fortunate, feeling that they need to slither out of one church and into another, in the hope of finding a place where they can deal with their problem privately. Starting over in a new ministry, or even leaving ministry altogether, is the only way they know to handle the pressure.

A congregation has enormous impact on ministry families, not only when they experience crises personally but also when they deal with crises occurring in the lives of their friends and peers. When in 1998 Ed's mother was in her last days on earth, we experienced the full love and support of the congregation.

She had battled cancer for four years, wanting in the end only to survive long enough to attend our son's wedding in another state. But it was not to be, for she entered the hospital for the last time just before we left town.

Through that stressful time, we knew that we were carried often to the Lord in prayer. It was difficult to feel the complete joy of gaining a daughter-in-law and enjoy the festivities while we thought we might not get home before my mother-in-law's passing. We did make it home, though, and before she died she was able to see all her grandchildren, the new bride and a wedding video, and her nephew from Ireland who brought love from her four sisters and their families.

For three weeks, people in the church rallied behind us. They provided meals and housing for anywhere from six to twenty-four people in our family. They took care of transportation costs for some traveling family members and gave many other tangible and intangible expressions of support. Our entire immediate family was with Ed's mother when she, in peace, took her last earthly breath. As expressed in the lyrics of Don Wyrtzen's song "Finally Home," we knew she would wake up breathing new celestial air in glory and would realize she was truly "home."

Ed and I have also experienced the loss of friends in ministry. The family of one dear friend has granted permission to relay their story in order to illustrate the blessings poured on us by our church.

Truman Dollar was a ministry acquaintance of Ed's during the early 1970s, and he gradually became our friend and Ed's confidante. Ed was with Truman and Donna Dollar when their formerly prejudiced white church opened the doors to African-American Christians in a town known for racial tension. Ed was also there on the day that Truman resigned from the ministry. Truman, a member of our church for his last eight years, took his own life in March 1995. Because Truman and Donna were members of Calvary Church, and because the church had prayed for them through a restoration process after Truman left the ministry, Ed told the congregation about the circumstances that led to Truman's highly publicized death.

After a memorial service in our church, Ed helped with Truman's funeral in Kansas City, Missouri. When he returned home, the day before Palm Sunday, Ed decided to preach the same message to the congregation that he had at the funeral. It dealt openly with all of the questions and emotions that loved ones face when people commit suicide.

A few people wrote letters to Ed expressing their displeasure that he had not delivered a "proper" Palm Sunday message. Dozens more, however—through notes, phone calls, and personal talks—indicated the opposite. Most notably, four people seriously contemplating suicide approached staff members for help. Many others dealt with long-buried grief, grief that they had hidden years before when their own loved ones had died. One woman visiting our church for the first time on Palm Sunday morning with her fiancé was, as a result of hearing the message, able to forgive her first husband for taking his life. She was able to take this step in time for her upcoming marriage.

We learned that many more people than we'd ever been aware of had suffered through a painful experience of this sort. One friend I'd known for over twenty years wrote to us about her first husband's death; we had not known that he had taken his own life. Many people were so relieved to be able to talk at last about their hard times with people who had experienced a similar grief. And Ed and I shared their feelings of guilt, the questioning, the anger, and the sense of betrayal so characteristic of this kind of event.

A congregation's sensitivity during times of grief and sadness can strengthen ministers in their resolve to continue ministering to others. The congregation serves as a surrogate family when extended family does not live nearby, or if spiritual ties to them are not close. Our own congregation supported us in so many ways. A few people advised us to take time to mourn and expressed the hope that we would work through the necessary steps of our own grief rather than move on quickly in our desire to minister to others. And some professionals offered an ear if we needed one. A Haitian proverb states, "Love is an active verb." As believers, we offer to God our "bodies as living sacrifices" as a "spiritual act of worship" (Rom. 12:1), and we can act in love when our Christian siblings hurt. In our case, members of the congregation proved their love in the wonderful ways they supported and helped us at that time.

We can give thanks that crises like this do not occur often. But in order to support one another in times of devastation, we must minister to each other every day—laypeople to each other and to pastors, and pastors to everyone. Paul said he "constantly" remembered the Roman Christians in his prayers (Rom. 1:9–10); he urged them to "join [him] in [his] struggle by praying to God for [him]" (15:30). Even in the early church, ministry was a two-way street. Leaders and followers offered refreshment to one another—like springs in the desert.

## Chapter 8

# THE SPRING THAT NEVER DRIES UP

"As for me," said Samuel to the people of Israel, "far be it from me that I should sin against the Lord by failing to pray for you" (1 Sam. 12:23).

Like Samuel the prophet, ministers of today have a responsibility to pray for the people whom God has called them to serve. Paul told the people in the church at Thessalonica that he, Silas, and Timothy prayed for them, thanked God for them, and remembered in prayer their work of love and "endurance inspired by hope in our Lord Jesus Christ" (1 Thess. 1:1–3). In church staff meetings, praying for the believers and unbelievers whose lives are being touched by the ministries of the church is always an item on the agenda. In Paul's second letter to the same church, he said again that he was thankful to God for the brothers, "because your faith is growing more and more, and the love every one of you has for each other is increasing" (2 Thess. 1:3). The prayers of ministry leaders include offering thanksgiving for the people, and for what God is doing in and through their lives.

The believers' response to Paul's ministry was to become imitators of their ministers and of the Lord. Likewise, the recipients of ministry need to pray for those who are ministering. The Thessalonians "welcomed the message" and "became a model to all the believers" in spite of suffering (1 Thess. 1:6–7). Their faith in God became "known everywhere" (v. 8).

In chapter 2 of 1 Thessalonians, Paul continues to enumerate specific things that his ministry team did, and he commends the church on its loving response. The ministers encouraged, comforted, and urged the Christians; the believers accepted the message as God's word. Paul mentions again their suffering for Christ's sake (2:12–16). As a true giant of the faith, he knew that his ministry was solely dependent on God's will, and he asked the recipients of his letters to pray for his spiritual and physical well-being (Col. 4:3).

The best and most important thing church members can do for their pastors is pray for them. People who periodically let their pastors know that they pray for them help to build them up spiritually and emotionally. All ministers rely on prayer support and often are aware of it during times of need.

During Ed's first year as pastor of Calvary Church, a godly man came by each week to pray with Ed. The man did not do this because it was his duty as a board member—although he was on the board; he did it out of love, and he continued to minister regularly to Ed for years.

Sometimes a gift can be given as a symbol and a reminder that the giver is praying for the pastor. A couple in our church was particularly struck with the need to pray for Ed when they heard that Palm Sunday sermon after Truman Dollar's death. This calling led them to give us a most unusual gift. On a tour in Israel, they bought a beautiful sculpture that reminded them of us. The sculpture is a depiction of Moses' hands being upheld by Aaron and Hur while Joshua was leading the Israelites in battle with the Amalekites (Exod. 17:8–15). As long as Moses held up his hands, the Israelites prevailed—but when Moses grew tired of holding up his hands, Aaron and Hur came alongside him and helped him. This couple wanted us to have the sculpture as a symbol of their prayers and the prayers of others for us. Each time we look at it, we are reminded that someone (many someones) pray for us often and regularly. We are encouraged not to be "weary in well doing" (2 Thess. 3:13 KJV).

While many people may wish to pray on behalf of their pastors, they may be unsure of what to pray about. In fact, those compelled to pray might never know why the Spirit prompted them, and they may never know the outcome of their prayers. Nevertheless, when we feel prompted to pray we should certainly do so. Sometimes we might find our pastors continually on our minds or we might keep running into them unexpectedly. We might keep thinking of their names. Any of these things can be taken as a holy signal to pray for them.

Still we may wonder why we should pray for pastors. After all, they are the ones who are supposed to be in touch with God. They are even paid to be! A pastor's library shelves likely contain several volumes on the subject of prayer. Ed has dozens! Put simply, God's Word encourages Christians to pray for their ministers. And knowing what specific prayers would benefit our pastors helps us understand why we should pray for them—as well as helping us remember to do it regularly. Here are some things to pray about:

1. *Thank God for the minister.* Several New Testament writers requested prayer for themselves. Paul said, "We always thank God for all of you, mentioning you in our prayers." (1 Thess. 1:2). Since he was thankful for the people in the church, it would stand to reason that churches could and should thank God for their ministers.

2. *Pray that pastors will teach the Word.* Later in the same letter, Paul states, "Brethren, pray for us" (1 Thess. 5:25). Because Paul was instrumental in starting churches in different cities, he experienced a variety of challenges regarding the culture and customs of each area and how they affected the daily activities of the

church. Worldly pleasures enticed people to hang on to their old lives. Paul and other church leaders needed constant prayer as they taught believers godly living. In 2 Thessalonians 3:1–2 Paul asked that the brothers pray specifically "that the message of the Lord may spread rapidly and be honored, just as it was with you. And pray that we may be delivered from wicked and evil men, for not everyone has faith."

3. *Pray that pastors will resolve any conflicts they might have with colleagues*. Paul's reason for requesting prayer may have included the relationships between missionary travelers and church leaders. He had been left by John Mark and had parted ways with Barnabas (Acts 15:36–40). Like Paul, people who are called by God today are not immune from conflicts, either. Often the mission of the church can be overshadowed by strong personalities and power struggles.

4. *Pray that the pastor will be open to change*. Not all conflicts in leadership are bad. They may simply indicate that change and growth are occurring and need to be recognized.[1] This may have been part of the reason for the division of Paul's ministry team. Even though conflict caused the split, the change may have been necessary for expansion. The leaders continued to minister in different regions. (Conflict resolution will be addressed in a later chapter.)

One day I was driving and listening to Christian talk radio. Several people were discussing the topic of change in the Christian life. One person said that Christians, whose lives should be marked by constant growth, are often the most resistant to change, especially when the church attempts new ways to relate to people. How true! Some people have even told me that change is impossible, to which I always respond, "And what about the biblical concept that 'with God all things are possible'?" Any method that has helped us with our behavior or spiritual growth was probably once a new idea. And if we read God's Word with the intent of being taught by the Holy Spirit, change in our lives is inevitable. Keeping change in mind, then, when praying for ministry leaders is appropriate. Without change we can neither repent nor grow, and none of us want to bear the eternal consequences of anchoring our souls to our present condition.

5. *Pray for godly wisdom among our church leadership.* Pastors, as well as staff and lay leadership, need wisdom in dealing with generational differences, cultural divides, theological challenges, spiritual immaturity, and interpersonal relationships. Churches must develop a relationship with the community and earn a reputation for integrity in legal and financial matters. Even though pastors may not (and should not) make all the decisions with regard to financial matters, people in the church should pray that their leadership will emulate wise, biblical principles.

6. *Pray that love and friendship will develop among coworkers.* Ministry leaders who genuinely care for each other should take the time to become friends. If their only contact is in the boardroom or through interoffice memos they are missing the benefits of loving "one another deeply" (1 Peter 1:22; 4:8). Paul demonstrated a loving relationship with Timothy as he mentored him.

7. *Pray that the minister will have a "clear conscience and desire to live honorably in every way" (Heb. 13:18).* A sense of honor and a clear conscience are important for all Christians. They are especially important for those whose lives are to be examples for others—those who lead believers and witness to unbelievers. Pastors and their families need to have open, honest business dealings with people in the community so they do not bring dishonor to the name of Christ.

8. *Pray for the pastor's family.* Probably the most endearing words Ed and I hear and the most encouraging notes we receive are those that pledge to pray for us and for our children. Whenever people tell me that they pray for our family, I thank them sincerely, tell them how much we need their prayers, and ask them to continue.

Whether offered daily, weekly, or in a moment of prompting by the Holy Spirit, prayers are needed and appreciated. For many years, I have enjoyed the fellowship of a group of mothers who come together to pray for each other's children. The other mothers know my children very well, and I can share concerns with them that I cannot share with everyone. I am thankful, too, for all the people in our church who pray for our children, even though the children may not know them. That is one of the ministry perks. Many people pray for us, both those we do not know well, and those we know well enough to ask for personal requests.

My husband used to introduce our family to the church on Christmas Eve, but generally speaking we were seldom seen all together as a family at church. Now, with some children out of the home and attending another church, we continue to appreciate people asking what our children are doing so that they can pray more specifically. In churches where the pastor's family members may be on the platform for various reasons, just seeing them is a constant reminder for members to pray.

9. *Pray that the pastor will read the Word of God with the intention of obeying it, and that he will resist temptation.* About 250 men from our church attended Promise Keepers. Many, following up on a challenge to pray for their pastor, called Ed's office to ask what he would like them to pray for. Ed has told his secretary to respond with the above request. He has given the request to many people through the years who have asked the same question. He is unable to disclose every area of his life that needs prayer, but he is acutely aware that the most important thing he can do is to love God and obey His Word.

10. *Pray however you feel led.* "You are sensitive to the leading of the Holy Spirit, and just the fact that He brings someone to your mind prompts prayer. Even if you do not know why you are prompted at a given moment, pray anyway. Pray however you feel led, and the Lord, through His grace, will translate your prayer to meet the pastor's or family member's need." This is

what I have said to the many people who have asked me how they might pray for our family. Like my husband, I cannot always think of a particular area that needs prayer. But people who are in tune with the Spirit will pray anyway. I may ask them to pray about a specific burden or about an upcoming event such as a speaking engagement for which I need special wisdom.

The lives of pastors are complex. Detailing a list of special needs to a person the pastor does not know well may be misinterpreted as a "to-do" list for God that everything might "go well." And, in truth, we would all be less likely to grow if everything always "went well." Just as wandering in the desert humbled and tested the children of Israel, so desert experiences humble and test us. Further, if we did not experience them we would miss the opportunity to consider it pure joy when we face trials of many kinds (James 1:2). And remember, even in the worst of desert experiences God's love and actions met the Israelites' everyday necessities—food, water, and clothes that didn't wear out!

11. *Pray that God will be glorified through the pastor's marriage, and that their relationship will not hinder the spread of the gospel.* Because God instituted marriage before sin entered the picture, couples forever strive for the ideal with their own earthly, imperfect attitudes and behaviors. Quite possibly nothing delights the Enemy more than destroying a ministry marriage. The fallout is wonderful! Not only are the lives of two people ruined but so are the lives of their children and their parents. Possibly other marriages might be influenced. And if Satan ruins a ministry couple's marriage, there is a real possibility that some people will decide to give up on church, reading the Bible, and believing in God altogether! Church members should pray earnestly and regularly that their pastor's marriage remains strong, even if the particulars of their relationship are unknown. Pray that they will resist inappropriate thoughts that could lead to sinful behavior. Pray particular Scriptures for their spiritual

strength, such as Ephesians 6, which urges putting on the full armor of God.

Ministry couples have compelling reasons to keep their marriage vibrant, besides their own sake and that of their children. Their divorce would bring shame to their ministry and the couple's loss of influence would hinder the spread of the gospel. They need to protect their marriage by continually building trust, sharing in one another's spiritual growth, and sacrificing for one another's welfare.[2]

12. *Pray that the pastor will be attentive to his wife's godly insight.* Ministry wives report that few stresses wear on them as heavily as that of emotional stalking, particularly if the target is their husband. Transference, which was addressed in chapter 2, takes a particular toll on wives. Sometimes a wife becomes aware, long before her husband does, that a woman in the church is trying to gain the pastor's attention.

One pastor thought his wife's warnings about another woman were unfounded until a couple in the leadership of the church came to him. They had noticed the woman's constant presence and felt that he should be warned. He was ashamed, then, that he had not taken his wife's cautions seriously. Once he was aware of the problem, he was able to prevent it from becoming more serious. The problem continued for many years, but the pastor's marriage only grew stronger.

People whose spiritual lives have been guided by male leadership probably have not given much thought to the challenges faced by female clergy. Often, a woman's sensitivity to relationships, however, allows her to spot potential problems. One pastor wrote about her discussions with peers about "power, depression, and the fine line between spirituality and sexuality."[3] Although she did not expand on the subject, I was reminded of former pastors we have known, who crossed that fine line. It started with legitimate listening and counseling sessions. In the end, it turned into ugly affairs that messed up their lives and the lives of their families, hurting thousands of people in the process. Church members would do well to pray that their pastors manage to avoid even the appearance of evil. And pray, too, for ministers who are unjustly accused of crossing the line.

13. *Pray in order to join the pastor's struggle.* In Paul's letter to the Roman church, he requested that they join him in his struggle "by praying to God" for him (Rom. 15:30–32). By praying for the one who ministers to them spiritually, believers can actually become part of the ministry. Joining the struggle means helping bear their minister's burdens, praying that he will be equipped with the full armor of God (Eph. 6) to fight spiritual warfare. By praying about specific struggles, members gain an understanding of what is required of ministers.

Members should also pray for missionaries who live in countries where political unrest is an ever-present danger. Many missionaries face the real possibility of death, and they and their families are in constant danger. Recognizing and living amidst these perils is a standard part of the commitment. New believers, too, in some countries face severe religious persecution. Pastors in Nepal, for instance, will not baptize believers unless they promise to obey God for the rest of their lives, even if that may mean giving up their lives for His sake.

America presents dangers of a different kind. Member should pray for pastors who minister in areas where gangs pose a danger. Church members in these areas often lose loved ones in drug-related killings, and the lives of pastors and their families are sometimes under threat.

14. *Pray any Scriptures that would be appropriate.* In *Praying the Scriptures,* Judson Cornwall writes, "God's Word petitions us to pray for the leaders and workers who have been given to the body of Christ. Reading these scriptural petitions in our prayer time will inspire us to pray for our own pastors, teachers and spiritual leaders."[4] In the following passage from Colossians 1:9–12; 28–29, the minister's name could be inserted.

I pray that _____ will be filled by You with the knowledge of Your will through all spiritual wisdom and understanding. I pray this in order that he may live a life worthy of You and may please You in every way: that he will bear fruit in every good work, growing in the knowledge of You, being strengthened with all power according to Your glorious might so that he may have great endurance and patience, and joyfully give thanks to You, who have qualified him to share in the inheritance of the saints in the kingdom of light. I also ask that he will proclaim Christ, admonishing and teaching everyone with all wisdom, so that he and other ministers may present everyone perfect in Christ. Help him to labor to this end, struggling with all Your energy which so powerfully works in us.

We can pray that we, like Paul, may desire to know Christ (Phil. 3:10). In the same way, we may pray for our pastor, "that he may know You and the power of Your resurrection and the fellowship of Your sufferings." Many passages in Scripture can be personalized so that we can use them as we pray for the leadership of the church. For example, several years ago someone wrote a letter to Ed saying that he prays for the pastoral staff of our church. He enclosed a copy of one of Andrew Murray's devotionals, which had prompted him to pray "for the preacher that he may speak 'in the demonstration of the Spirit and of power,' and . . . for the congregation and for ourselves, that we may receive the Word, not from man, but as it is in truth, God's Word, 'which effectually worketh in you that believe' (1 Thess. 2:13)."[5]

Sometimes people learn that their prayers are answered—but often the benefits of prayer are unknown. This, however, is no cause for discouragement, because God gives us enlightenment just often enough to increase our faith and strengthen our desire to pray for others. Often when Ed and I sense a need for support, people will tell me that they have been praying for us. Even when I cannot share details, I encourage them to continue—because we truly need and count on the prayers of God's people.

When a prayer warrior goes home to heaven, I always pray that God will raise another to take his or her place, that He will put a burning desire to pray in the heart of a believer—one who will take it seriously, and who will indulge in it regularly. And in His marvelous way, God is already answering that request even before I know that I need to pray for it.

Ed used to fish with a man about fifteen years ago, but we had had no contact with him since then. Recently he met with Ed again and told him that he still prays for our whole family every morning. What a treasure! When our family leaves one church and goes to another, we may think that most people have stored us away in a memory bank or put us in an old photo album on the shelf. But even if only one person continues to remember us in prayer, they have covered us with God's blanket of protection, love, and power. By becoming prayer partners with their ministers and praying for them, believers know the peace of doing God's will in that area of their lives.

In studying the life of King David, I was fascinated by the accounts of the men who came to David's rescue in the heat of battle (2 Sam. 14–22; 1 Chron. 20:4–8). David was not a sinless man, but God used him as a shepherd, warrior, king, and leader. David had a small group of valiant soldiers who risked their lives for him and stayed with him when others deserted. Would it be stretching the analogy too far to say that pastors, too, need a few loyal friends who will stick by them no matter what takes place in their lives? Prayer—through all battles and hardships, and accompanied by accountability, steadfastness, and a large measure of grace—would surely prevent a lot of pastors from church hopping. If pastors preach God's Word and try to live out what they teach, the ones to whom they minister should stand by them, uplifting them with prayer (vertical) and helping them with practical support (horizontal).

One Tuesday morning in the prayer room of our church, one of the women told us she had visited her son's church in another state. She had adapted from that church's bulletin a prayer for the preaching pastors of the church, and she requested that we read it together as a prayer. It is presented here with blanks for inserting your own pastors' names.

## Confession for Pastor _____

Father, in the name of Jesus, I thank You for giving _____ Church pastors after your own heart; shepherds who feed us with knowledge and understanding.

I pray and confess that your grace rests upon Pastors _____ in full measure. I declare that the Spirit of the Lord shall rest upon them; the spirit of wisdom and understanding, the spirit of counsel and might, the spirit of knowledge, and of the fear of the Lord.

Pastors _____ are anointed to preach the good tidings to the meek; to bind up the brokenhearted, to proclaim liberty to the captives, and the opening of the prison to those who are bound. Thank You, Father, that freedom of utterance is given to them and they open their mouth boldly and courageously as they ought to get the gospel to the people. As Pastors _____ teach and preach the Word, revelation knowledge flows freely. Their speech and preaching are not with persuasive words of man's wisdom, but in demonstration of the Spirit and of power. Pastors _____ live pure and holy lives before both God and man. They are men of faith, integrity, wisdom, honesty, and compassion. They're above only and not beneath; they're the head and not the tail;

they're blessed going out and coming in. They prosper in all things even as their souls prosper. They reign in life by One, Jesus Christ.

In the Name of Jesus, I pray that Pastors _____ will submit to You and resist the devil and that he will flee from them. I pray that no demonic forces sent to attack my pastors and their families will have success, because greater is He who is in them than he who is in the world. I pray a hedge around their prayer and study time, their time with their families, and their times of rest and relaxation. I surround them with the Name of Jesus and the Word of God. I declare that no weapon formed against them can prosper and any tongue that rises against them in judgment will be shown to be in the wrong. They are hidden in the secret place of the Most High under the shadow of the Almighty whose power no foe can withstand. The Most High, the Almighty God is their God, their refuge, their fortress in whom they safely trust. They are hidden in the secret pavilion from the strife of all tongues.

I confess that Pastors _____ (and spouses' names) have marriages that exemplify Christ's love for the church. (The spouses' names) are virtuous women and their price is far above rubies. They are precious in God's sight because of their gentle and peaceful spirits and in our sight as they do their husbands good all the days of their lives.

I confess that I will stand with Pastors _____ and their families and undergird them in prayer. I will say only that good thing that will edify, encourage, and protect them. I honor Pastors _____ as men of God and will continue to intercede for them and declare blessings upon their lives. In Jesus' name, Amen.

When I read the line *I will say only that good thing that will edify, encourage, and protect them,* I burst out crying. Many things were being said in the church at that time that were neither edifying nor encouraging. Without any prompting, the group of women surrounded me and prayed for me. When they returned to their seats, one by one each confessed their own sin in some things they had said. It was an awesome moment, because I had thought few people knew how much they could discourage a pastor by their words. God's presence was evident in that room. The unity of our spirits brought great joy as well as a renewed commitment to live by the Word.

*Chapter 9*

# AID FOR WEARY TRAVELERS

"Most (ministry families) will move at least three times during a ministry career, staying at a church an average of five years."[1]

I sometimes imagine that moves in the ministry are like the travels of the Israelites (Exod. 40:36–38). When the cloud of the Lord lifted in those days, they moved; if it did not lift, they did not move. While it is true that people in ministry who are living obedient, godly lives do not want to move without God's guidance and direction, the similarity probably ends there. For the Israelites, the carefully planned layout of the tribes and their families ensured that the whole extended family moved together at the same time, with everyone having responsibilities as they pulled up stakes. But, while I believe that God is pleased if my spirit is willing to move to another ministry when His "cloud" lifts, in practical terms ministry moves are not so simple.

Even if the circumstances are positive, moving is often painful for people in ministry. The ministry couple has invested their hearts in the congregation, and it can be agonizing to leave. In some denominations, a pastor is called from one congregation to another every few years, creating upheaval in the life of the family. And just because the move is a result of God's call to another church does not nullify the difficulty of adjusting. Some wives, although willing to follow the Lord's leading with their husbands, feel as if they are abandoning their flock. The hurt can be even worse if the congregation does not express its own sorrow upon seeing the pastor leave. It is understandable that when members learn that the Lord is leading the pastor to another church, they don't want to say things to make the pastor's family feel guilty. "Better that they cry than applaud," one wife said. "But silence is loud, too."

For some ministry wives, the cycle of moving creates a feeling of alienation. A ministry wife who is grieving over the church she has just left finds it hard to open herself to the people in the new church who are eager to receive her. With time she heals enough to begin new friendships. By that time, however, parishioners who have sensed her withdrawal might not open themselves again to her for years. Then, if the pastor thinks of moving to another church, his wife may agree it would be just as well since she's never felt included in this flock! If she feels different emotionally from her husband whenever they move, she may be exhausted from starting over and over in each new city. And if she finds herself in a tight rural community, she may find breaking into the circle is even harder.

And there might be other problems. Several ministry women report the trauma of leaving a nearly adult child behind in a ministry move. The mother can feel that her whole identity has changed—the family is no longer whole. One family left a church after having served there many years. They moved to a new part of the country, sent a child to college in another state, a second child to another country, and had only one child left at home. This mother felt stressed when people complained, a month later, that she should have settled into the community by then. She had not shared what was troubling her because she did not want anyone to feel sorry for her.

According to a couple who mentor ministry couples, changes are in general emotionally harder on the wife than on the husband. His new work is exciting for him, and he can easily forget that his wife is finding the change heart wrenching. She often shoulders the added work of making address changes, taking care of medical records, changing doctors, dentists, and all the other business contacts, while her husband whistles off to work. In attending to the details of a new home and neighborhood, she will miss the personal contact that her husband is able to enjoy through his involvement with people in the church.

The husband, however, does not entirely escape the emotional disruption of a move. A move, no matter how positive the reasons for it are, always entails loss in that the pastor must say good-bye to a familiar life where he had his bearings. He must immediately begin to minister to people who are dealing with loss while he may still be experiencing his own loss. Most ministers and their families try to find and experience joy in spite of and through these losses. Finding joy is an essential part of following Christ. It is not good enough to simply endure.[2]

I have observed ministry persons changing churches so often and quickly that I cannot help but wonder if the moves are caused by restlessness or discontentment. If I, an "insider," am curious about frequent moves, it would not be surprising if the general church population was also curious. I am reminded of Aslan, the Lion in the Chronicles of Narnia. Several times he is asked why certain events happened to others. "I tell no one any story but his own," Aslan responds. This is known as C. S. Lewis's "doctrine of privacy."[3] It is enough to know that the Lord expects us to obey His leading. Although sometimes we cannot help but be curious, and curiosity in itself is not a sin, we need not know why things happen to other people. When I am tempted to dwell on the private matters of others, I remind myself of Peter's question to Jesus regarding John: "What about him?" Jesus simply said, "You must follow me" (John 21:21–22).

All of us in the family of God would do well to remember

this when leaders come and go. We are all growing, even those in ministry. We are placed and replaced where and when God needs to do a work in our hearts and in the hearts of those to whom we minister.

Just as ministry families are sometimes upset at being moved, so are church members when staff come and go. Some ministers are not in a church long enough for people to build trust in them. On the other hand, even during a short stay, members may become well acquainted with their leader and look on him as a friend. The layperson "left behind" is sorry to see the pastor and family leave and may not want to get to know the next pastor fearing the possibility of losing another friend.

Angie, for instance, was a teenager who felt upset and abandoned when three youth directors "passed through" their church during her high school years. "Mom," she cried, "what is wrong with us? Nobody wants to stay with us!" Angie did not understand the reasons for staff changes, and she felt a need to connect with ministry people during that important and exciting time of her life. She was, of course, not alone. Other teens felt unwanted, and their parents' hearts ached for them.

Members of a congregation may live their whole lives in their hometown; a ministry family rarely has that experience. Thus many members may not identify with or be aware of the disorientation associated with frequent moves. How, then, can church members help the incoming ministry family, as well as themselves, adjust? How can they make the changes positive and of spiritual benefit? The way that a minister and family initially acclimate to a new church community will, in large part, depend on the church's readiness for them. Board members can help by becoming personally involved in the adjustment. A great deal of the preparation should be done by the board who, through informational meetings, can advise the congregation about the new family prior to their arrival. Also, the board can address concerns and answer members' questions.

By the time a new minister moves into a community, issues such as theological outlook, leadership style, and ministry involvement will already have been settled between the search committee and the candidate. If the church has been looking for a pastor for some time, and the search committee is agreed, the relief of ending the process will create a joyful atmosphere. If, however, there has been division in the search committee during the process, the strain may be felt for years by the incoming pastor. The board should be open and honest about such conflicts, both with the new pastor and with the parishioners. Hiding certain facts can hurt.

One pastor tried for years to figure out why some families in the church remained emotionally distant from him. He finally asked board members some very direct questions. He found out that during the search some people had skirted the church's mandated process by inviting another man to visit as a candidate. Hurt feelings and anger lingered long after the new pastor had arrived on the scene. He had sensed this disunity but did not know the cause. The governing board of the church could have helped the new pastor and hastened their own healing if they had been forthright in revealing the circumstances surrounding his call. Hiding church problems is not the responsible way to deal with them. The new pastor could not lead them all to greater spiritual maturity without knowing the source of bitterness.

Sometimes members or staff who have helped support and guide the church during the search process are reluctant to give up their authority when the new pastor arrives. The power struggle continues until the pastor breaks and leaves, or recognizes the game and gives the board an ultimatum. Unfortunately, churches that break one pastor seldom stop with one. (Thus the need for caregiving ministries for clergy described in chapter 5.)

Under more positive circumstances, the arrival of the new pastor gives church members who love to "do something" opportunities to exercise their talents. While they help the new minister's family, they lay the foundation for future friendships. Many pastors' wives report that, when relocating to a new church, they received a genuine outpouring of tangible love.

Ed and I started our first church in 1973, and about a year later we bought our first home. We held an open house to celebrate with members of our congregation and served a bit of food. People surprised us with "housewarming" gifts—some even as practical as kindling wood, complete with demonstrations for a couple who had never started a fire.

Before we moved to Grand Rapids in 1987, my husband commuted for several months until school ended and the home we were buying was available for possession. We received dozens of letters from people in the new church; realtors offered assistance in finding housing; people with children our children's ages sent greetings and pictures to help us become familiar with names. We even received an "I love Michigan" refrigerator magnet.

On unloading day in Michigan, eight women washed all the walls and curtains, and several men helped by hanging an antique porch swing and installing appliances. Someone also rented a steamer to take feminine wallpaper off our son's bedroom walls. Other women brought food, while several families took our children away from the confusion for a time of fun. The day after the movers finished emptying the truck, two women unpacked kitchen boxes while another (after asking my permission) washed every item and organized the cupboards, drawers, and pantry. Professional people who attended our church offered their services, and schoolteachers from our district introduced themselves. All of this friendliness helped us meet people and seemed to confirm to us that we were doing the right thing.

We bought a home in Michigan thinking that we would quickly sell our home in Virginia. A full year passed, however, before that happened and, during five of the months, the house was rented for substantially less than the mortgage payments. Although the church was generous in moving us and in helping us get into our home before we sold the house in Virginia, none-theless, making two house payments was tough. At a time when selling the house in Virginia seemed only a bleak possibility, a couple in our church sent a check for slightly more than a month's mortgage payment. We were profoundly grateful for the gener-osity and hard work of our new congregation. All incoming pas-tors should be so blessed.

Many pastors and their families struggle as they settle, whether with family problems or financial adjustments. Whether the pastor and family are moving into a parsonage, apartment, or their own home, church members can offer the same kind of help that the people in Grand Rapids so generously gave us. If the new minister and family accept the offer, a designated per-son can find out what they need or want done and what jobs they prefer to do themselves. Helpers, too, should be sensitive when discussing with the family any specific expectations or regulations the church may have about the parsonage.

Church members can facilitate the integration of the pastor's spouse into the church community. They can offer to take the couple's children to a special event with other children their own ages. They can host a "women only" luncheon for the pastor's wife or a get-together for young moms and children at a park.

There will be many jobs that need to be done and errands that need to be run when a pastor and his family try to make a new place feel like home. They will undoubtedly appreciate genuine friendliness from helpful people. Members of the congregation who are uncomfortable doing this type of work can assure the ministry family of prayer support or offer referrals and specific information about the town. The help of church members does not shield the ministry family from problems, nor can it solve them. But stepping in to support the pastor's family can be an uplifting and cheerful experience for all involved.

# Section 3

## ENCOURAGING YOUR PASTOR

## Chapter 10

# MAIL CALL

## The Power of the Pen to Uplift Spirits

Dear Pastor,

Our thanks for a powerful sermon on a most difficult subject. We thought we were okay in our thinking
and didn't really have a problem. However, as your message unfolded we found areas where we have been
deceived! Thank you for pointing out what Scripture
really says so that we can seek God's forgiveness and make
the necessary changes in our attitudes.

Ed received the above letter after he preached a sermon on
prejudice. These mature Christians did not consider themselves
beyond growth in their faith and took the time to tell him that
they had been prodded to make changes. Possibly nothing—
besides being with people when they repent and trust Christ as

their Savior—delights a pastor more than hearing that his preaching and teaching of the Word has made an impact in the lives of
believers. The couple who wrote the note added this prayer:
"Lord, give us a sincere desire to try to understand rather than
condemn."

Writing notes is an enduring way to encourage your pastor.
By letting a pastor know how the Word is changing your life,
you may become an "angel of mercy" in a time of stress or tragedy. A note can affirm and invigorate the pastor's commitment
to proclaiming Truth clearly. Also, it encourages accountability
on the writer's part. Putting a change of heart into words nudges
the writer to follow through with what he or she has written.

Short e-mail responses to missionaries' prayer letters lets
missionaries know that they are not completely ignored or forgotten. Some people called to ministry, both in America and in
other countries, labor a long time before ever winning a single
soul to Christ. It may be years before they even perceive a change
of attitude. The labor seems worthwhile if someone "notices"
and cares in a note.

Not all letters, however, have to be "spiritual" in tone. Even
"men of the cloth" have a sense of humor! We have kept and
laminated cartoons people have sent to us that illustrated or poked
fun at something Ed did. Ed used to play a gutbucket, a home-
made instrument made from an upside down metal tub. One
end of a piece of rope attaches in the middle of the tub, and the
other end is tied to the top of a broomstick held by the "percus-
sionist." Plucking the rope creates a sound slightly akin to a bass
fiddle. It is a funny enough contraption to begin with, but Ed's
facial expressions while playing it have been the brunt of quite a
few funny notes. A tall seminary student sent a gift to Ed. My
husband is . . . well . . . not tall, and the student sent a poster
that read, "Ed's Too Short." Truth is, Ed's Too Short is the name
of a band.

Laughter is sweet medicine; laughing at ourselves is preventive medicine. If we can laugh at our own idiosyncrasies we are more likely to be gracious toward those of others.

Church attendees who live in areas where Christian radio is available have no doubt heard of Pastor Appreciation Month. Some dear people have written us wonderful letters of encouragement, simply because it was Pastor Appreciation Month. Some have said that they had been intending to write for a long time and finally could put it off no longer. Because it takes time and effort to express appreciation at any time of the year, notes always mean a lot.[1]

Christmas cards and letters are also a thoughtful gesture, but they arrive at one of the busiest times of the year for pastors. I read a few cards to the family at mealtime each night, but there are usually so many that we are rushed. So I keep them in a large basket, then later in the winter we enjoy reading them carefully by the fireplace.

Whether on stationery or a card, by e-mail or "snail mail," a full page or just a few lines in length, a note of encouragement to your pastor or to his family is always appreciated. If what you say is sincere, it is never in poor taste.

## Chapter 11

# MEAL CALL

## *The Joys of Hospitality*

One of my friends taught in a parochial preschool. One day, she was telling the children what work nuns and priests do on a daily basis. A boy raised his hand and said, "But what do they eat?" Some of you may have wondered that about your minister. The answer is "food."

A biblical example of hospitality appears in Acts 16. A jailer is saved after Paul's and Silas's chains were miraculously loosed. He "brought them into his house and set a meal before them; he was filled with joy because he had come to believe in God—he and his whole family" (v. 34, author's translation). Joy was experienced both by the host and by the guests that day. The same can be true today when people share meals, especially in their homes, with others.

As Christians, we all have a responsibility to entertain strangers (Heb. 13:2) and to be hospitable to our neighbors. Philemon, who opened his home for a local church meeting, was commended by Paul for refreshing the hearts of the saints (Philem. 2, 6). Hospitality is a way to open our hearts and homes and to minister to people—to those we know, as well as to strangers. The epistle of 3 John is written to Gaius because of his hospitality to brothers in Christ whom he did not know. John tells him that "we ought . . . to show hospitality to such men so that we may work together for the truth" (v. 8). I know some missionaries who spend a great deal of their time entertaining other missionaries and ministry people who are traveling; they feel it is part of their calling. And yet, when they come home to America, they themselves are seldom invited into the homes of people in their supporting churches. Webster's dictionary defines "hospitable" as being "given to generous and cordial reception of guests." It is disheartening and disappointing that many of us in America are so wrapped up in our own schedules that we do not take opportunities to be hospitable.

Although hospitality is certainly a gift, it needs to be addressed as an issue separate from gift giving or honoring, since there are so many possibilities for creativity in offering it to the pastor and family. Most families are busy, but there are few things that will be appreciated more than inviting someone—whether in ministry or not—to your home for a meal with your family.

Some of the best times for Ed and me have come through spontaneous invitations, not only from church members but also from families of our children's friends. Spur-of-the-moment plans sometimes work better than booking times together weeks or months in advance. Our children have often enjoyed these times far more than we could have predicted. Their lives and ours have been enriched by the opportunity of getting to know people through this personal touch.

Do you have qualms about offering hospitality to your minister? You are not alone. Some people never invite their pastor to a meal, not only because they think he and his family are too busy but also because they have too lofty an idea about his "office." They forget that he is a normal human being who, like everyone else, needs regular meals. Some people are afraid of serving something the pastor does not like or cannot eat. Even worse, some people feel that their kitchen must be redecorated first!

The truth is, too many of us worry too much about the appearance of our homes and use that as an excuse not to have visitors. When one of our missionaries to Africa was on furlough, she spoke to a group of women from our church. She mentioned that the people she serves are so very hospitable. She repeated a Nigerian proverb: "How you show your face is more important than how you spread your mat." In other words, relationships are more important than appearances.

That Nigerian proverb may have had biblical basis. Jesus taught the same concept to Martha. She was "worried and upset about many things, but only one thing [was] needed. Mary [had] chosen what [was] better." Mary sat at the Lord's feet listening to what he said (Luke 10:38–42). Martha was hospitable in opening her home to Jesus, but she wanted the mat spread just right. Mary was more interested in intimate communication with Jesus, and He did not deny her that opportunity by sending her off to the kitchen to help with preparations.

Yes, it is practical and courteous to put away clutter, to clean the floors, sinks, and toilets of any bathroom that a guest may use—but it is not essential. The master bathroom shower does not have to sparkle if the pastor is coming only to the kitchen for coffee! We need to lighten up and shoot for tidy, not spotless. Serve what you have the most experience making or what your family enjoys the best. The pastor's family probably does not fix gourmet meals every night at home, and they certainly do not expect them in homes where they are guests. If you think it will help you feel more comfortable, invite a close friend to join the group or even to help with the preparations.

Through all the planning, we should remember that opening the heart and the home are important; how the home looks is not. If you want to host the pastor's family, remember they are human. Chances are not everything in their kitchen is perfect and not every meal is served in formal style.

Here are a few tips for extending an invitation to the pastor for a planned meal:

1. Offer several possible dates. If someone calls us with an invitation and our calendar is full, I simply ask the host if another date would do. Have before you a list of the dates that are not possible for you, and ask for the same information from the pastor—or, more likely, his wife. Allow time for her to check other family members' calendars and the church calendar and get back to you with an answer.

2. If you wish to entertain couples only, consider whether your request will place a hardship on the pastor's wife in finding a baby-sitter or transportation for children's activities. Offer alternative plans that might make the event easier for her.

3. Make certain you are clear about whether the whole family or adults only are invited. If your church pays a very small salary to the pastor, offer to pay their baby-sitter. The same should be true if you sponsor a daytime meal or event and expect the pastor's wife (or any other moms of young children) to be there; always take the rest of the family into consideration, especially if the children are small.

4. Unless your minister has made it clear to the congregation that he does not wish to be sociable, assume that he has the same social needs as everyone else in the congregation. Some people are surprised to find that their minister may be interested in car races, sports, or many other hobbies that their own family likes.

5. Inform the pastor's wife whether the dress is casual or not. Whether you plan to wear blue jeans for a barbecue or formal wear for a Christmas dinner, you will not want your guests to be embarrassed by not being dressed appropriately.

6. Remember that the pastor and his family like to have fun. Don't assume that all the pastor is capable of discussing is theology. That presumption alone would keep people from wanting to entertain their pastor! We have a few friends we always call when we need some good laughs. They understand, although they are not in ministry, that sometimes we need a few lighthearted hours to lift our spirits, and their kitchen table is the very spot where we can spend them.

Some communities are so close-knit or closed that they will never invite an outsider to their homes. One couple I know who has ministered for over forty years in one place are still outsiders. They have never been invited to other people's homes, even though they themselves are very hospitable. They have learned to accept the community as it is, but the reality of it has often left them lonely for fellowship through the years.

Some people may feel intimidated about inviting their pastors into their homes but would venture something outside them. Entertaining away from home is always an option—in a restaurant for a meal, at a park for a picnic, or on a boat for a ride.[1] If the hosts have special thoughts or circumstances they wish to share with the pastor's family, this can make the time together especially meaningful. Sincerity is the best door opener.

One of the nicest invitations I ever received was from a doctor's wife. She invited us to spend a day at the cottage they were renting. And this is the part that endeared her to me. "Come," she said, "even if your husband is working. I often have to attend social events without my husband, so I know how nice it feels to be welcome without him."

That is a good invitation to give single pastors, too. Everyone likes to feel they can contribute to a conversation, whether or not there is a spouse present. Widows of pastors often experience neglect, because so much of their social life centered around their husband's position. For this reason, I encourage pastors' wives to make some contacts outside the church. Then if their husbands are suddenly taken out of the ministry for whatever reason, they are not totally at a loss for companionship.

People who attend large churches probably think that the pastor must be invited to hundreds of meals a year. This is not necessarily the case. It is possible that so many other people are thinking the same thing that the pastor and his wife have not been invited out for months.

During our early years in Grand Rapids, when our children were young, many families invited us to their lake homes in the summer for picnics and boat rides. Then a few years ago, our youngest child, Daniel, informed me that he had not had a boat ride all summer. I realized that the children of most of the families who had invited us to their boats were now fully grown. I scrambled to think of someone who would not mind taking Daniel out, and who would not think our whole family had to be invited. The man I asked made Daniel's whole summer! He picked him up at our house, drove him to the cottage, and let him be captain of the boat on Lake Michigan!

A comment that I hear—and likely other pastors' families do, too—is, "You are so busy." That is true, but if I have too much going on to schedule an event at a particular time, I try to make time later. May and December are busy months for pastors who have children in school. It is helpful if hosts keep that in mind when issuing invitations. But even then, there are often days or evenings that are free, and we usually can make time for things that we want to do—especially if it is eating a meal!

Reaching out to people through hospitality, whether to strangers, acquaintances, friends, family, or pastors is always a two-way ministry. Although the hosts takes the time and effort to make food and fellowship enjoyable, both the hosts and the guests receive refreshment for their souls merely by being together. If a close friendship develops as a result, that is a bonus—but hospitality should not be offered for the sake of gaining friendships. More likely than not, the hosts and guests will find many areas of common interest to keep the conversation alive.

Age differences do not need to be a factor. Ed and I have developed a deep love for three people much older than we are because of a memorable meal. Shortly after Calvary Church extended a call to Ed to become the senior pastor, we came to town with the whole family. A retired couple invited our family, along with a widow friend of theirs, to their home for a meal. I panicked when I saw the table set with a beautiful white linen cloth and fancy china, but the hostess assured me that Daniel, two years old at the time, would be fine sitting in an old high chair she had kept through the years. All was well until Daniel started eating the red Jell-O. He felt nuts in it and decided that foreign objects should not be tolerated. He started spitting. There was no tray on the high chair, so Ed cupped his hand to catch the falling debris. Daniel did not stop spitting until every bit of chopped nuts was expelled from his mouth. We apologized profusely to the hostess, who cheerfully assured us that everything was washable. The story has been retold many times, and we can laugh about it now. But it was not funny that night!

Neither was the time a new friend invited us for Sunday dinner. She had graciously asked me what the children liked, and I had told her. She served roast beef and gravy, potatoes, and carrots. Out of the blue, Daniel announced that he "hated cooked carrots," while I turned the color of beets. In another home, Heather asked me if the potatoes were instant. I softly told her to eat whatever was passed; she loudly refused to eat them because she "hated instant potatoes!"

So take this chapter with my warning: If you extend hospitality, be prepared for anything to happen. It just might.

*Section 4*

# ENGAGING YOUR PASTOR

# Chapter 12

# MOTIVE, TIMING, AND GODLESS CHATTER

*A word aptly spoken is like apples of gold in set-
tings of silver.*

—*Proverbs 25:11*

Ed was born in Northern Ireland and grew up the son of a pastor. It was not until he became a minister himself that his father told him something that used to happen after every Sunday morning service there. For seven years, Ed's dad greeted people at the door as they left the church. Every Sunday, a man said to him in the same angry tone: "Well, you got *that* off your chest." In 1964, when Ed was fourteen, the Dobson family emigrated to the United States. On one of their return visits to the church in Belfast, nearly thirty years later, the man apologized.

## Motive

Psychotherapists could analyze what motivated that man to greet his pastor in such a confrontational way for so long. In fact, we have tried to come up with a few good reasons ourselves, but speculation has led us nowhere. We can be thankful that most people do not speak to their ministers like this, although some cannot seem to find the right words to say. "Congregations consider themselves church families, and most truly do care about their pastors. . . . Because they care so much, members of the congregation want to communicate with their pastor. Trouble is, they don't always know how to do it effectively."[1]

Bear in mind, however, that whatever you say to your minister has the power and the potential to build him up spiritually and emotionally or chip away at his will to serve. Words can rejuvenate a minister, or they can deplete his reserves. When addressing our pastors, we all need to be clear about our motives.

A writer tells the story of a pastor who received a phone call complaining about something he had said during the Sunday morning service. The caller had truly misunderstood and had spoken hurtfully and legalistically.

*"What made it even more vexing was that the complainer was an 'established' saint, one who had walked with the Lord for many years. Someone of that much experience should have more understanding, greater tolerance, and certainly more grace. But they decided to speak up without considering the effects of their call. It may have made them feel better to get it off their chest, but the consequences far outweighed the benefits. It makes you want to stop trying,"* said my associate.

The writer goes on to say that if most people took a little time to consider what it is we are really trying to accomplish and the effects of our words on that desired outcome, we would simply stuff much of what we say to each other and never say it. Our objective is simply and clearly stated in Hebrews 10:24–25, "Let us think of one another and how we can encourage one another to love and do good deeds. . . . Let us do all we can to help one another's faith." We want movement in a Godward direction, even if we think it could have been done better, even if the effort was less than perfect. [Ministry people] can't prevent everyone from throwing cold water on a starting fire.[2]

# Timing

Timing is not everything, but it is critical. Through trial and error, most people learn that timing is important. People who call their pastors or approach them face-to-face are usually more concerned with the point they want to make than with their timing. Everyone thinks that his or her point of view is correct, and that it needs to be conveyed *now!*

Regardless of what we might want to discuss with our pastor, a little common sense about when to initiate the conversation is always in order. If the subject is important and needs to be discussed in our home, some times are better than others. When Ed is exhausted from preaching two or three services in a row, I decide which matters can wait and which need immediate attention. In other words, if I want to have a cheerful, two-way conversation, the Sunday dinner table is not the time to discuss a problem in the household.

Church attendees, too, should consider timing when they have something important to discuss with their pastors. As a minister heads for the platform, his mind is focused on his message or on the prayer requests he is about to share with the congregation. Asking what he thinks about the resignation of a favorite football coach is better left for another moment.

If churchgoers are unsure about the importance of their topics for discussion, writing them down and thinking about them will help to clarify what should be urgently brought to the pastor and what can wait until a more appropriate time.

# Godless Chatter

Church members can help the pastor to be obedient to Scriptures. Paul warned Timothy that, as a pastor, he should "guard what has been entrusted to your care. Turn away from godless chatter and the opposing ideas of what is falsely called knowledge, which some have professed and in so doing have wandered from the faith" (1 Tim. 6:20–21). The pastor's calling is a serious, weighty matter, and the people of the congregation would do well to refrain—even in jest—engaging their ministry leaders in "godless chatter."

We are not told exactly what godless chatter is, but Paul's admonition to Timothy is an excellent caution to everyone. I have used the principle of godless chatter to teach children that what they watch on television sometimes causes them to think and talk about sins as if they were funny. I have very little knowledge of recent cartoon shows, but the *Flintstones* is a good example. The two married couples in the show connive against one another, lying in the name of teaching one another lessons and making "put-downs" between spouses appear normal. While watching another cartoon, Daniel once asked me what a voodoo doll was. I explained and then asked, "Is it being presented as something funny?" It was, and the television was immediately shut off.

These examples may seem off track in a discussion about guarding our pastors from conversations that might tempt them to disobey Scripture. But by practicing ways to guard our attitudes and words at home, Christians can teach their families how to relate to their ministers about spiritual matters. Not everything we say to our pastors needs to be serious or specifically about religious, spiritual, or theological matters. We should be careful, however, about making light of godly or satanic matters. In fact, all Christian conversations should be sifted through scriptural principles, not just the ones we plan to have with our pastors.

Perhaps an even stronger warning about godless chatter can be found in Ephesians 5:4, 12: "Nor should there be obscenity, foolish talk or coarse joking, which are out of place, but rather thanksgiving. . . . For it is shameful even to mention what the disobedient do in secret." When someone starts to tell Ed a joke, and he can sense the way it might go, he asks if the subject is racism or immoral behavior. If it is, he says he does not want to hear it.

> *When words are many, sin is not absent,*
> *but he who holds his tongue is wise.*
> *—Proverbs 10:19*

At a ministry conference a ripple of laughter floated through the room full of clergy. The speaker mentioned a "certain someone" in every congregation who can always be counted on to say the wrong thing at the wrong time, to criticize no matter what the issue, and to complain no matter what pains are taken to prevent offense.

Avoiding godless chatter when engaging our pastor in conversation does not mean we should never criticize. Nor is it godless chatter when we make those occasional slips of the tongue that cause our faces to turn red. We have all said the wrong thing on occasion. But a wise person (and it is hoped that a teacher of God's Word falls into this category) is "full of mercy" toward others who are known for their slips of the tongue.

Many of our words, though, are thoughtless, idle chatter. Some dear brothers and sisters, for instance, think that their gift of discernment bestows on them the right to criticize and complain whenever they feel like it. Someone recently said to me, "Nothing is safe from criticism when you're around Christians." How sad. Constant complaints directed to pastors can eventually pull them down and deflate them; a barrage of criticism may be the final twist of the knife that causes a pastor to think, "What's the use?"

We know that "pleasant words are a honeycomb, sweet to the soul and healing to the bones" (Prov. 16:24). Yet how many times have we peeled, chopped, shredded, and boiled a person before considering that passage? An idle put-down of a minister may be meant as a joke, but someone overhearing it may take it seriously, which could forever alter that person's image of the pastor. It might even lead the person to seriously doubt the pastor's character.

When I was a child, my mother warned that speaking ill of the pastor was the same as laying a hand on God's anointed. She was referring to the story of David warning Abishai not to harm Saul while he was sleeping (1 Sam. 26:11). People in ministry are as human as anyone else and subject to the same failings. Yet extreme caution should always be taken in voicing comments about someone in ministry.

Nor should ministry people themselves be exempt from this caution. Some of the faxes and e-mails between friends who work in churches are nothing but gossip, careless words for which an account will be given: "For by your words you will be acquitted, and by your words you will be condemned" (Matt. 12:37).

Ministry and laypeople alike need reminders to tame their tongues. Much godless chatter is presented as something that one feels "led" to write or say. It would be a good idea if the church could institute a spiritual gag order that would prohibit participants in any church controversy—be it doctrinal or otherwise—from discussing their viewpoint with the pastor or anyone else. Only incontrovertible or undeniable facts would be permitted in the discussion. In truth, everything else is damaging. And it is sadly true that, in the Christian community, so much that is spoken is damaging. Most of my young life was spent watching people whose spiritual lives were based on the differences they had with their own brothers in the Lord. I often wondered why their darts were not aimed at the real enemy—Satan—or why their attention wasn't drawn to the planks in their own eyes (Matt. 7:3–4).

When Jack Wyrtzen (founder of Word of Life Camps, Schroon Lake, New York) challenged me to love and witness to everybody, I determined to develop a genuine love that would extend to everyone. How could I love people who needed to be saved, then turn against them if they, as Christians, did things differently from the way I did? Would I spend my life arguing with my Christian family or dedicate it to telling people about Christ's love? I wanted to know more of God and to live a Christian life that did not limit the fellowship in His family. I decided that people should not be rejected if they did not talk or look or even behave like the rest of the family.

Talking to those who minister to us about our thoughts and feelings can affect our whole demeanor. The way we communicate is like a light that shines out onto people who do not know the Lord. We may be able to recite Scripture. We may give unbelievers information that the Holy Spirit will use to draw them to the Savior. But when vulnerable new believers see the way we treat our ministry people, are we leading them to spiritual maturity or to spiritual doubt?

## Chapter 13

# TALKING FACE-TO-FACE WITH YOUR PASTOR

People called to ministry usually have not experienced every kind of trial. Neither can their training equip them to minister effectively in every kind of circumstance. God does, however, teach and mold every one of His servants in ways that will allow them to feel His presence and become more empathetic ministers. Grief, suffering, and humbling experiences will all work together to shape those who dedicate their lives to serving the Lord. If a congregation recognizes that growing through trials is a necessary part of their pastor's spiritual journey—as well as their own—they will adjust their expectations to allow for this growth. That recognition will also affect the way church members perceive their pastor when they approach him with a problem. Perceiving even a beloved, godly pastor as a human on a spiritual journey allows for grace. Grace is the giving of something—love, forgiveness, gifts—out of our own goodness and not based on the recipient's worthiness. The extending of grace by church members to their pastor does not come about automatically. It must be cultivated as a spiritual discipline and applied to all Christian brothers and sisters.

Christians seldom realize the magnitude of their words: "The tongue has the power of life and death" (Prov. 18:21). The tongue can deceive, crush spirits, break hearts, inflict stabbing wounds, separate friends, and kill a minister's will to serve. The tongue can also dispense grace. It can promote healing, understanding, and love. It can protect, give joy, spread good news, and teach knowledge (chaps. 12–17). Understanding the importance of the content and motives of our speech can show us how important face-to-face interaction with the pastor can be.

Tom was asked to be the interim pastor of a church. He and his wife, Joan, had just been informed that their grown, unmarried daughter was pregnant. The child was to be placed for adoption, and they would be losing a grandchild. Tom felt that the board of the church should be made aware of the situation. While he shared the information with the male leadership, Joan told the deaconesses about the trial they were facing. Unlike some churches that might have rejected a pastor whose family was in crisis, this church embraced Tom and Joan, recognizing their profound grief. One deaconess whispered to Joan that now she could admit that her own son was in jail. She had been fearful of judgment and rejection until then. Not long afterward, an older couple in the church invited the pastor and his wife to their home for dinner. There they shared their own grief; the same thing had happened to them many years before. Through the years they had kept it a secret. In this sad situation, the congregation became more open. The people began to bond with each other, and this paved the way to new healing and a ministry to others. Members felt they could open their lives to their minister, and they shared their own struggles and heartaches. Because they did not condemn him, they knew he would not condemn them.

When a pastor faces trials similar to those of the people he ministers to, the congregation's respect for him does not need to diminish. A church community that demands perfection from the pastor and his family is spiritually immature. In the situation mentioned above, people were actually empowered when they embraced the trials of the pastor's family.

Relating appropriately to the pastor on a daily basis, however, is just as important as doing so during crises. For most church members, that day-to-day relating is done face-to-face. The question is usually whether to schedule an appointment or simply catch the pastor at an opportune moment.

Most pastors make themselves readily available, particularly to those who are in crisis. But this availability often leads to abuse by people who do not want to "bother" calling the office or feel they do not want to wait a few hours. Pastors and their families understand the occasional member who catches the pastor for a few moments when he is between activities. Some members, however, appear to be compulsive. And it is the chronic compulsive callers who test the patience of every ministry family I have known.

Because at certain times (such as before a Sunday sermon) pastors need to remain focused, it is recommended that people who have personal matters to discuss call the office for an appointment. An emergency—imminent death or sudden serious illness—is, of course, an exception. Routine callers should also consider whether the matter they wish to discuss could be better handled by another person on the church staff. Often the senior pastor will find he needs to refer them to someone else.

If the caller is trying to get in touch about a routine matter, the pastor's need for a private life should be taken into consideration. The pastor is a real person, in and out of the church. Yes, he will jump out of bed to meet a family in need, but the pastor needs rest, both mental and physical. In a large church where many crises seem to come in big waves, the pace can be exhausting.

Some pastors spend a lot of time counseling, and some refer parishioners to other professionals. In either case, a person can be assured of confidentiality. If someone tells a pastor his or her intimate story, it will not be shared with a mutual friend or be used as a sermon illustration. Although most people assume that the pastor will not broadcast their secrets, some may think that the pastor tells his spouse everything that has been covered during an appointment. I am puzzled when people assume I know what they discuss with Ed.

A wise person will make good use of the time scheduled with the pastor. Granted, a person in crises is mentally distraught, but in most cases it is helpful to keep discussions concise. If the pastor or secretary has indicated a time limit on the visit—"The pastor has forty-five minutes on Wednesday"—that time frame should be respected. If necessary, additional meetings can be scheduled.

It is unfortunate that this kind of constraint has to be a part of our lives. Ed and I are seldom able to take time for relaxed and unhurried conversations with members of our church, and we regret that. We do enjoy those special times when we can and plan them as we are able, but time always seems to be a factor. As a result, people who attend our church do often perceive us as "too busy." In spite of that busyness, however, and the large number of people who make up our church body, we have come to know and love hundreds of people, and we continue to meet and become acquainted with even more.

Even in a small church, members of the congregation should respect the pastor's schedule as much as possible. Just because a church does not have many members does not mean the pastor has nothing to do with his time. Our experience is that, whether Ed was the only staff member—opening and closing the building, cleaning, teaching Sunday school teachers, leading the choir, visiting, preparing and delivering messages—or whether he was working with a ministry staff of seventeen and custodial and support services as well, the pressure, stress, and hours invested were much the same.

The pastor and board have a responsibility to make the times that the pastor is generally available known to church members. Then they will be less likely—save for emergencies—to interrupt private times for studying or disturb family time.

Even during regular work hours, there are good and bad times to communicate with a pastor. Because my husband has gained a reputation for being approachable, people sometimes want to give him immediate feedback after a service. He does not mind speaking to people who have a genuine need and who seek him out instead of going to the prayer room. But an untimely critical remark can destroy his ability to focus on what he has to do. Ed usually preaches more than one service on Sunday morning, and he often has an additional one at night. If, during the next service his thoughts keep shifting back to the displeasure someone has expressed earlier—no matter how kind the approach—he can easily lose his concentration. That happened one Sunday. Ed arrived home ten minutes earlier than usual. He was sure he had left out a point of the sermon!

Whether a pastor speaks once a week or many times a week, if churchgoers can wait for an appropriate time to articulate their complaints the pastor will be able to focus better. If criticism is constructive, he will most likely be able to assimilate it with the right spirit.

It is often a good idea to consider why criticisms are made at all. Churchgoers may want to say something friendly, but cannot think of an appropriate greeting that doesn't sound trite. Then they blurt out whatever has been on their minds, however inappropriate that may be. While Ed and I were standing in a store aisle, a woman whom we had never seen before approached Ed and said, "Well, I'm glad you got a haircut; now I can finally listen to the sermon!" Then she walked away. We shook our heads and later we both wondered, "What is she *really* angry about?"

It is also well to remember that the pastor does not have absolute control over every facet of church life. Many issues within the church—whether concerning leadership, youth ministry, or musical preference—are never completely laid to rest because of generational and cultural differences in the congregation. Yet many people think that the pastor must know every detail of every problem in the church and that he can fix it by giving an order. Micromanagement of church operations is not always feasible and certainly not biblical. In many churches, staff, elders, or lay ministers have responsibilities in areas such as choosing "psalms, hymns and spiritual songs" (Col. 3:16). If members have concerns about these matters, it would be more effective to approach the appropriate people. The pastor can then give attention to "prayer and the ministry of the word" (Acts 6:4). Many pastors, however, walk into their offices on Monday morning feeling downcast. The last words they hear from members on Sunday nights are complaints about music or someone's failure to wear a tie on the platform. How uplifting it would be for those pastors to hear positive feedback from members about the work that God is doing in their hearts through the Word.

## "Tell Pastor . . ."
## —Face-to-Face or Secondhand

Some people think that if they cannot catch the pastor and do not want to schedule an appointment, they can pass the word to his family members. This indirect approach may save time, but if the "word" is critical or carries an agenda, it causes stress for the messenger. He or she may feel manipulated.

I am thrilled when people tell me what they appreciate about my husband and his sermons. I love carrying messages that brighten his day. I love it when someone says to me, "Ed hit the nail on the head! I felt like he was preaching just to me." Then I know that not everyone thinks the sermon topics are meant for "somebody else," or that someone wishes the pastor would force people to live according to their own preferences. It is good to know that some people react by saying, "Ouch!"

Some comments, however, simply wear on my spirit: "I'm glad he shaved his beard"; "He looks sick, thin, and tired"; "It looks like he's lost weight." Many pastors' wives field comments like these, and we try not to take everything seriously. It is amazing that people still think that wives should take charge of our husbands' lives and see that he gets his hair cut or wears matching socks. We can be helpers but are not called to be controllers.

If people approach me about serious matters, though, I often recommend they call my husband at the office or ask his secretary for an appointment. On occasion, I am reminded of the biblical principle that we Christians are to go to brothers who have offended us. The Bible does not state that we should ask our pastor's spouse to pass on our criticisms. I try to practice that biblical principle when I have a concern, and I encourage others to do the same. (More of this topic will be covered in chapter 15, "Not the Best Way.")

Music is the issue that people in the church most often ask me to discuss with Ed. Many people know that I studied music, and they think that because of this I pull more weight on this subject with "the pastor." In reality, it is the minister of music who has the difficult task of trying to give people a taste of many styles of music. Music is closely tied to our emotions, and it is always a hot spot among many Christians.

I think I understand how people feel on every side of the music issue. Many years ago a choir I accompanied was learning an antiphonal piece of music with biblical words. One choir member, Thomas, did not know the history of church music, and he had never sung any style closely related to classical music. He thought that the church was no place for it. He even expressed hatred for it! Over many weeks, the music director taught the music section by section, giving some elementary theory instruction and distributing devotionals related to the text. In the end, Thomas actually enjoyed performing it.

So, please, I beg you to reconsider when you are tempted to ask your pastor's wife to tell her husband any of the following: we sing too many praise choruses; we don't sing enough songs out of the hymnbook; we stand up too long; we left out my favorite verse; we sing too many old songs; we sing too much classical music; we should stand more often in reverence to God.

One can only guess why people ask the pastor's spouse to pass on a message rather than approach the pastor face-to-face. Perhaps they lack the courage of their convictions. Perhaps, too, they like Thomas lack the courage to accept change. The more I study, interpret, and apply the Bible to life, the more I realize that it is all about change—changing to conform to the image of Christ. Changing my will in obedience to *anything* God teaches me from His Word. The changes called for in the Bible may have nothing to do with music, but at times it might. People dig in their heels about their pet theories, and no logic, new perspective, sermon—not even God's Word itself—will change their minds or hearts. I know this is true, because I hear people say it often. "Change isn't hard," they say. "It's impossible." And it frightens me for them. Sometimes I want to reply, "Don't you have any fear of God for the consequences of refusing to change?" Howard and William Hendricks wrote,

> Many Christians are like poor photographs—overexposed and underdeveloped. They've had plenty of input from the Word of God, but what difference has it made in their lives? Spiritual growth is a commitment to change. And yet, the human heart resists nothing as strongly as it resists change. We will do anything to avoid it.[1]

May God help us to see that our theme song must not be "I

Did It My Way." Step by step on the journey, we must try to do everything His way, even if we have never done it that way before.

## Face-to-Face—Third Hand

"Remember, you're the pastor's son/daughter!" Some people give their messages to a pastor face-to-face. Some pass their messages through the pastor's spouse. Some even pass their messages through the pastor's children. And make no mistake, the statement above is a message. It directly relates to the pastor and his spouse. It is a message aimed at the heart of their parenting.

Ed and I try to model godly behavior. We try diligently to teach our children to do the right thing. We do not tell our children, for instance, to be polite to others because their dad is a pastor but because being impolite is a sin. Once we asked our oldest son not to attend a school junior high activity. We were not absolutely sure but felt that the activity itself might be wrong. We did not want his presence to become an offense to anyone else and, frankly, we did not want others to wonder why a "pastor's son" was allowed to attend the event. It was a difficult decision and there was no Scripture to give us clear instructions. We decided to err on the side of caution. Our son complied, and as we sorted through this and other issues with him he realized that we did not say no to him without just cause. After he graduated from college, our son told us that, even though he was by no means perfect in his adolescent behavior, often his behavior was influenced by our attempt to live godly lives, and the fact that he did not want to hurt us. As a mom, that still makes me cry!

When people tell my children to behave because their dad is a pastor, they imply that we should use Ed's calling as a stick to control what they wear, what they do, who they hang out with, and how much they should be involved with the youth group. We try to teach them to wear clothing that is appropriate for the occasion, and we teach them the importance of discerning God's leading and of getting involved in ministry as God leads them. This is much healthier than teaching them to do the impossible—please everybody.

As Christians, our most important task is to grow in our relationship with Christ. Adults often burn out in ministry because they expend too much energy trying to meet other people's expectations. Ed and I have tried to let our children be children—not "preacher's kids." But, in the eyes of some, they will always be PKs.

Jill Briscoe wrote an article about preacher's kids specifically aimed at ministry women. I think several points may also be useful for laypeople. Based on God's Word and our experiences, we parents in ministry try to give our children the "armor" they will need for the battles of life. But, like David, many children recognize that they cannot wear Saul's armor. They want to and need to be themselves. "Was David's character the worse for struggling to find his identity as he was constantly treated like a 'nobody in a house full of somebodies?' If he had not been left alone to face the lion and the bear, could he have ever stepped out *alone* to face Goliath?"[2] Not only did he fight Goliath, he did it in front of all Israel—which the author compares to the church!

As ministry parents, we must allow our children to wear their own armor, to choose their own weapons, and go off to battle leaving us at home to pray. And pray we must. We can pray that they will choose the armor of God (Eph. 6). Praying for the pastor's children—instead of telling them how to behave because their dad's a pastor—is the best thing you can do for them.

Many times people come to the wrong conclusion about the pastor's children because they listen to incorrect information. When one of our children was disciplined for breaking a rule on a youth group activity, only one person out of potentially hundreds who knew about the situation called to say that she was praying for us. Six months later, another person called to ask if I needed a shoulder to cry on; she had *just* learned about it, along with a significant amount of additional wrong information! Our child learned some valuable lessons: one unwise decision can have long-lasting effects; misinformation can never fully be explained to everyone who hears the wrong story; and many people do not care about the truth.

We cannot control gossip. We can only pray that, in time, our children's lives will speak for themselves. We have no power to make our children mature in the Lord faster than the children of laypeople. Neither are we perfect parents. We struggle through problems with each child, and we pray for God's wisdom when we make decisions.

Communicating face-to-face is an effective and personal way to express God's love for brothers and sisters in Christ. Pastors and their families ask only that, when a message is conveyed, it be delivered to the appropriate face.

*Chapter 14*

# TALKING WITH YOUR PASTOR ON THE PHONE

People who enter ministry know they will be on call twenty-four hours a day. It is part of the calling. When a church board hires a pastor, it likely expects that the pastor will be readily available to the congregation. People would not enter ministry if they did not truly love people and want to minister to them whenever they are in need. The challenge for those in ministry is that a 24/7 job wears on the body, soul, and mind, as well as on every facet of family life. It goes with the territory.

A child murmured, "Stop talking," as his mother talked to the pastor after church. Pastors' children may sometimes feel like saying that to their parents, too. They understand, however, that talking to people after services is part of their parents' lives. Many pastors' children grow up waiting for their dad and mom until the very last person leaves the church. And sometimes people talk to the children until their parents have to pull them out of the building! Most ministry families understand that talking to people is a major part of ministry life.

It is almost impossible for pastors to get away completely from their work. But most pastors agree that observing a weekly Sabbath is not only a matter of obedience to God but also is essential for maintaining balance. Just as laypeople need to take care of their homes or their personal business on their days off, so do ministers. Pastors may just want to enjoy being at home, reading or doing nothing. This does, however, leave the dilemma of the telephone. Many pastors report that people call them at home on their days off so as not to bother them at work!

Sunday is Ed's busiest day. He talks to people, delivers sermons, keeps a demanding schedule, and generally tries to stay "up." So Monday is his day to crash. On that day, Ed usually begins studying for the next Sunday, and his day off is Thursday. Most people in our congregation know this and, except for emergencies, they are considerate enough to refrain from calling him at home on these days. Whatever day your pastor takes off, try to understand that, unless you have an emergency, it would be better to wait until another day to phone. Many pastors' wives actually tell people who phone on his day off that he cannot take the call.

I am grateful for the thoughtfulness of the majority of people in our congregation. They often apologize for calling our home when there is no need for them to apologize—we would be upset if we were not informed about their circumstances. Occasionally, someone from the church will actually ask if members are sensitive enough about phoning Ed at home. They are truly interested in knowing whether people give us the space we need as a family. I wish that every ministry family were so blessed.

Many people who attend church do not seem to realize that no single person can be available all day, all night, all month, all year without being worn thin emotionally and physically. Granted, when problems hit, church members do not have the luxury of scheduling an appointment for a conversation with their pastor in two weeks. But if pastors were to take every single phone call, they could find their health in a head-on collision with their ministries. No amount of protection by the pastor's spouse or the church board will completely alleviate the matter of phone calls. The pastor must monitor the problem himself.

But consideration by others does help in this never-ending challenge of ministry life.

Pastor's spouses understand the dilemma church members face: "When is the best time to call? I can never seem to get through to him at the office!" I'm sure almost every church has had problems with their phone system at some time or other. In the last few years, I have become increasingly sympathetic to people who call our home saying that they can get no answer at the church. I get frustrated myself when I call and get no answer, or when, after speaking to the receptionist, I get the voice mail of the *secretary* for the staff member I'm trying to reach. Communication technology makes it hard to maintain a sanctified attitude.

Yet when people call me thinking that no one is at the church, I encourage them to persist. If they call during office hours, someone *is* there to answer. Periodic glitches in the system are continually monitored and repaired. Now in our church, partly because I have mentioned this problem many times to church leadership, someone is available to answer the church phone on Saturdays as well as on weekdays.

Some smaller churches, however, may not even have an answering machine. Several years ago, we drove through the town in Virginia where we started our first church. Twenty-eight years ago, when we began meeting in the high school auditorium up on the hill, we didn't even think of secretaries, and voice mail did not exist. Today, with our lives consumed by technology, it is easy to forget the thousands of pastors and their families who are their own answering service. Though communication systems are different from church to church, people are the same. People have needs twenty-four hours a day, and they want the pastor—now.

If a church can afford a secretary, that person will most likely work a set schedule. The office hours can be posted in the Sunday bulletin, sent out in an informational letter from the church board, printed in the local newspaper and yellow pages, put up on a sign at the church office, or recorded on a telephone answering machine at the church. Having this information readily available saves many calls to the pastor's home.

A secretary will be the person best informed to schedule daytime appointments. When people call my husband at home about seeing him, he almost always says that he will have to check with his secretary and his schedule at the office. Chances are, if he agrees to something on the spur of the moment, he will have forgotten that something else has already been scheduled. Pastors should let their church members know their preferred way of scheduling.

Ministers want to be available to people. If they did not, they would not be in ministry. When private family time becomes a concern, pastors can work with the church board to block off time for study and for family. Disseminating information about personal time can easily be accomplished, even if the church has no secretary and even if the pastor studies at home.

People understand that their pastor's schedule may be full; though his ministry may be a calling from God, it is also his job. Pastors organize their time, as much as possible, to accommodate the needs and schedules of church members, but a pastor's children also have expectations—that their dads and moms will be attentive to their world. After all, most of the time their own world is all children can perceive.

Until the phone rings.

"Since pastor's not at home," said the caller, "maybe you can answer this question." I've heard this request dozens of times. More often than not, even if I have been able to give the requested information, the caller would still have preferred to hear it directly from Ed. Now when I hear "Since pastor's not at home . . . , " I tactfully suggest that the caller contact Ed at the office.

Many reasons exist for calling the pastor even though it may not be urgent. Thus, it would be beneficial to discuss phone communication with the pastor's family. Church boards may not realize it, but they are hiring "two for the price of one." And the rest of the family is part of the package as well. Family members, unprepared for the many circumstances that can lead church members to call the pastor at home, may inadvertently offend or hurt callers. This possibility places a lot of pressure on ministry families.

Pastors' spouses can often sense when a caller (whether connected with the church or not) has an urgent and genuine need for help. If the pastor is out of town, the spouse must decide how to respond to people in crisis. One person who called our home did not want to talk to an associate pastor because the caller's family did not know any of the staff other than Ed. Others have needed immediate comfort, and I did not want to say the wrong thing. On so many of those occasions, I have experienced God's help. He has reminded me of specific Bible verses and analogies that are helpful and appropriate for these families.

When Ed is home and I answer the phone, if I am unsure whether it is an urgent or necessary call, I always ask for the person's name before giving Ed the phone. If it still is not clear, I pass the receiver to Ed anyway, shrugging my shoulders to let him know that I do not know why the person is calling.

As our children have matured they, too, can often sense distress in people's voices. Our daughter Heather answered the phone one evening, after Ed and I were asleep. "Is pastor there?" asked a crying person. Because Heather was sure of the caller's distress, she knocked and came into our room to give the phone to her dad. Another time, a woman called and talked to our daughter for about twenty minutes. The woman had no idea how young Heather was and gave no thought as to whether her problem should be discussed with a pastor's child.

Our children are not at all insensitive, but they are not always emotionally or spiritually equipped to do anything substantive for people they do not know. Even with sensitivity training, however, children are children and cannot be expected to handle each call like a mature adult. When individuals call the pastor's home with no regard for the age or maturity of the one who takes the call, they may find themselves confused by the answers they receive.

Someone called our house about the setup of chairs and tables in a room at the church. Our son Kent, who had been away from home for three years, answered the phone. The caller mentioned a staff member's first name. Not realizing that personnel had changed and that the new staff member had the same first name as the former, Kent gave the caller the home phone number of the former staff person. For several hours a few people were very confused!

There is no simple solution to the ever-present telephone quandary. But the following questions may at least help you organize your thoughts, whether you call the pastor at home or at the office:

1. Could the question be asked during office hours? If someone's car is in a snowbank, it is after midnight, and that person cannot think of anyone with a truck to pull him out, it might be understandable if that person calls to see if the pastor can think of anyone to help. The pastor may not be the best resource, however, for finding someone a ride to church. In other words, think before trying to catch the pastor at home. By giving thought to timing and the information needed, a caller may realize that the call is not necessary.

2. Could a secretary, Sunday school teacher, staff member, or the pastor's spouse answer the question? Several widowers have told us their wives took a lot of information to heaven with them, most notably phone numbers! In general, a husband is not the person to call for a church member's phone number. Every time someone asks Ed for a phone number, he turns to me and asks, "What is so-and-so's number?" The most up-to-date—although not necessarily up-to-the-minute—information on members' phone numbers is usually available from the church office. Our church provides a directory of those in the congregation who wish to make their numbers available. It is *never*

complete or up-to-date, however, because constantly printing updates for general distribution is costly and time consuming.

3. Is it necessary that the pastor know the information you are calling with? Really necessary?

4. If people are given to calling the pastor on impulse, they would do well to consider how that may distract the pastor from his mission, main focus of ministry, or family. (I am not against making calls on impulse; the Holy Spirit *does* prompt people at times, in which case the situation is recognized joyfully as God's timing.)

5. Dilemma: The pastor's phone number is unlisted, but you need to discuss an important matter with him or someone in the pastor's family. Give the pastor's secretary (or administrative assistant) at least a hint why you are calling, and ask him or her to give your name and phone number to the pastor or family member. I have used this strategy many times when trying to reach businesspeople who attend our church. If Mr. Jones's number is unlisted (in the regular phone book as well as in our church's directory), I call his office and identify myself and my reason for needing to speak to him. When Mr. Jones returns my call, he can decide whether to give me his home phone number for future calls. People who have been harassed by unsolicited or rude phone calls are compelled to protect themselves with unlisted phone numbers. Pastors' families are no less susceptible. In fact, pastors sometimes receive death threats and must shield their families.

6. Church members should let someone know if they have a need to be seen or called by the pastor. Pastors are not mind readers. Some people feel they have been neglected by their pastors when, in fact, the pastor has not been made aware of the person's need. People have called my husband's office and asked his secretary, "Do you think the pastor or his wife would be willing to talk to me?" If Ed or I learn that a person with a serious need is hesitant to call us, one of us contacts that person immediately.

Even if Ed is already overloaded and dealing simultaneously with several crises, he is more likely to return a call promptly if he knows the reason for it than if he sees a phone message that says "Sister Blanchard called." We would feel distressed if we learned, after the crisis were over, that Sister Blanchard had not wanted to bother us or had assumed that someone else would inform us of her need.

7. Patience may be required. Sometimes we have to remind our children that we are expecting calls from friends and acquaintances, too! The teenagers in our home are the same as those in any other family, so we give time guidelines to our family. On some days, e-mail keeps the line busy for long periods of time. We appreciate people understanding this when they call our home.

Different families handle telephone courtesy differently. We have tried to establish certain rules in our family. The children do not say where their father is unless they know who is calling. They do not know where he is at every moment, anyway! "Would you like to speak to my mom?" is often the response. Because we are in ministry and receive emergency calls, we do not allow our children to put silly messages on the answering machine. We do not say our last name when we answer the phone nor do we put it on the answering machine greeting. Past situations have caused us to practice restraint in giving out information. The answering machine greeting gives our phone number and, because the number is listed in the phone book, the caller can then check his or her accuracy.

8. Callers should identify themselves. People who simply say, "I'm a friend," automatically raise suspicion. A pastor's wife knows her husband's real friends. When people tell my husband's secretary, "I'm a friend of Ed's," she often asks me if I know them before passing on the message. If a caller is afraid of being identified, they can say so and indicate if the matter is urgent. We have taught our children to identify themselves when they make calls and to ask callers to identify themselves before giving information.

One Sunday afternoon, in the days before caller ID, a man hung up on me when I asked him if he attended our church. He had given me his name so I looked it up in the phone book. I called him back and explained that knowing more information would help me help him. He was very polite then and told me the nature of his call, which turned out to be vital for our family. Obtaining information from a caller is sometimes as important as giving information.

9. There may be real reasons why a person "can't get through" immediately to the pastor.

a. The pastor may not be readily available. (He could be at meetings, out of town, keeping appointments, studying, or at a funeral home.) If the call is critical and the senior pastor is not available, the secretary can ask other staff, board members, lay ministers, or the pastor's spouse to offer aid until the pastor is available.

b. Some people think that if the pastor is not in the office he is at home. Others assume he is at home without trying the office first. When someone calls the house at midday, wanting to talk to my husband, I reply, "He's at work. Have you tried the church office?"

"No," says the caller, "do you have that number?" I squelch my urge to laugh and to reply that I do not!

10. The pastor's wife may not have read every book her husband refers to in his messages. A pastor's reference books are most likely at the church (if that is where he studies), so it would be logical to direct questions about them through the church office.

11. In a church where two or more pastors take turns delivering the sermons, it is common for callers to ask, "Is Pastor So-and-So preaching this Sunday?" I offer these guidelines:

a. Call the office during office hours.

b. Read the newspaper ad on Saturday.

If a caller's uncle is visiting from out of state and has always wanted to hear a particular pastor, the question is understandable. It is surprising, however, that many callers want the information to help them decide whether or not to attend the church at all that Sunday.

12. If a pastor is not at home, the spouse might not know whether the pastor is in the office at that particular moment. If the matter is urgent, the caller should indicate the nature of the call and allow time for the spouse or secretary to locate the pastor. In an emergency, every effort will be made to get the information to the pastor as soon as possible.

13. Don't be afraid of the answering machine. If your message does not require a return call, leaving a message on the answering machine saves time both for you and for the pastor. Even if the call concerns an emergency requiring immediate action, leaving a quick identifying message lets the pastor know someone tried to reach him at home. He may have been in the garage and missed the call by only a minute. Making use of an answering machine can be a lifesaver.

14. Church members can assume that their pastors go to bed early on Saturdays, and that on Sundays they are too focused or exhausted to hold lengthy conversations.

15. Pastors do not always want people to talk themselves out of calling. A spontaneous phone call to the pastor's home late Saturday or Sunday night can put a finishing touch on the day. One night Brian, a church member, called late. He had just talked to his stepfather, Carl. Knowing that we had prayed for Carl's salvation, Brian could not wait to tell us that Carl had prayed for forgiveness of sins and trusted the Lord for salvation. That was a call that thrilled us and was well worth making.

The kind of people who constantly call the pastor's home would not likely read this kind of book. Telephone courtesy lessons are wasted on them. However, most people are considerate. As has been mentioned before, we are all works in progress. We all make communication mistakes and need to have them brought to our attention. If love in Jesus Christ is the motivating factor, we will be encouraging and building each other up on the journey. We can grin and grow in our love for all. Whether we place a phone call at an inappropriate time or make other communication *faux pas,* what matters is whether we are striving to live in obedience to God's Word.

A few other matters related to telephone communication might be mentioned here as food for thought. Pastors often get requests to attend fund-raiser banquets from parachurch organizations. It is wise to find out from the pastor's secretary what his general feelings are about attending such functions. A number of years ago, Ed and I realized that we were hurting the feelings of some members of our congregation if we attended one group's banquet but turned down another's. If we attended one, people might see us there and remember that we had turned down an invitation to *their* ministry activities. Many causes— animal shelters, disease research, special needs groups—want to use Ed's name to lend weight to their organizations. With few exceptions—our church contributes to a shelter for battered women, and we attended the opening—Ed now declines this kind of invitation. Unless the congregation is small, a pastor would not have time to prepare sermons and respond to the needs of his congregation if he attended every scheduled function. Keep in mind that many churches hold men's ministry breakfasts, early morning Bible studies, social gatherings of Sunday school classes or youth groups, and fiftieth-anniversary celebrations, *in addition* to weddings, funerals, services, board meetings, and personal mentoring or discipleship meetings. Neither can the pastor's spouse attend every daytime and nighttime meeting and class. Just as church members who are involved in ministries within the church must balance their involvement with family life, so must pastors and their spouses. Parishioners who understand this are appreciated and allow the pastoral couple to experience joy as they minister.

When engaging your pastor, keep in mind once again that he is a human being and take into consideration what might be appropriate times for comments and conversations. When you meet your pastor to discuss church-related business or a personal problem, it is always appropriate to respect his position. But there is no need to overspiritualize every conversation. Remember, too, that pastors and their families are already familiar with the clichés about "the pastor," "pastor's kids," and all variations of the old pastoral jokes. It is easier for the pastor's family to communicate openly with people who do not treat them like spiritually categorized, stereotyped oddities of the church. Like everyone else, we are normal people who are still growing.

*Section 5*

# DISAGREEING WITH YOUR PASTOR

## Chapter 15

# NOT THE BEST WAY

This book could have been on the market two years ago if I'd known how to write this section. My rough draft ignored it completely. This topic has caused a great deal of soul-searching on my part and, frankly, I don't know how to address it without sounding like a whiner, but here goes. Christians sometimes disagree with one another. A number of conflict-resolution books are already on the market so I thought I could get by with skirting the issue. My godly publisher thought differently.

Disagreement is unpleasant, and I don't pretend to have all the answers. Nor do I wish to sound as if I'm defending my husband in some way or trying to tell people in the congregation what they ought to say and how to say it. The bottom line is that we Christians all need to grow up in the Lord as we try to work out disagreements with either church leadership or with our brothers and sisters in the Lord. Sometimes we do not really need to address disagreements at all. Sometimes what we need to do is to lay the problem before the Lord and remain quiet on our knees in prayer—especially in cases where we are not fully informed about the concern, and others can better deal with it. Before looking at how to disagree, we need to look at why we disagree.

If people decide to attend a specific church because they agree with its theology and practice (perhaps having read the church constitution), what would cause them to disagree with the pastor? In the first place, many people do *not* choose their church this way. For example, our church is beautiful, and engaged couples sometimes decide to attend it and become members so that they can get married in it. (Sometimes they change their minds when they discover the lengthy process for both church membership and marriage preparation.) Some people attend churches because their children are happy, at least for the time being, with the youth program or Sunday school. Others attend a church because they feel comfortable there. And, of course, many thousands of people attend a specific church because it is where their family has attended for generations. In other words, sentiment is often considered more important than what is preached and practiced, even though churchgoers may feel stifled, spiritually unchallenged, or even spiritually dead. One lady told me that she came to our church on Sunday nights because she needed to get some "meat from the Word." She belonged to a church that left her feeling flat, but she had no intention of moving her membership. Her family was buried there!

For whatever reason people attend a church, at some time or another they will likely disagree with something the pastor says or does. My husband has initiated many ministry programs and opportunities that have been the targets of complaint and criticism simply because "we've never done *that* before!" Of course, in a new church *everything* is new, and people are more tolerant of experiments in that situation than they might be in established churches. I think the theme of some churches is, "If it ain't broke, don't fix it!" "Broke," however, is not necessarily the best reason for change. Church leaders may feel the Holy Spirit breathing new life into their culturally outdated agenda, prompting them to take risks in the church and in the community.

There is the risk of being "taken" whenever a novel outreach program is initiated. Pastors reach out to people through different media, and their names can become well known in particular areas. Someone looking for attention (and ultimately grace, which "the world starves for") might contact a pastor and ask to share his or her story with the congregation.[1] The storyteller shares his or her experience, elicits sympathy from the congregation, then the story turns out to be untrue. As a result, the pastor receives an avalanche of criticism for neglecting to exert wisdom and discernment. Critics forget that any person may be deceived, and pastors are no exception; that is a risk we take in ministry. The pastor undergoing criticism may be tempted to ask his critics to reassess their own lives. Have any of us—lay or ministry—never needed forgiveness in the area of deceitfulness, manipulation, or leaving out part of the truth?

As for the pastor being the victim of deceit—part of the criticism from church members will stem from their own feeling of being "had." But when we are deceived by someone whom we have tried to help spiritually, we must not let a root of bitterness develop. We must guard against becoming cynical and critical. Far better to leave it with the Lord, respond with forgiveness, and move on. Yes, people will disappoint us. But we must not withdraw and decide not to give of ourselves again. Of course, if the community of believers has been unsettled about an outreach that has made it vulnerable to deceivers, they may respond with, "I told you so" and let the pastor know that it is time to get back to the "good ole days!"

If a pastor has a growing, successful-looking ministry, we might think he would never receive letters of criticisms. Bill Hybels shepherds a church near Chicago that is more than twice the size of ours. He averages about one negative letter per thousand attendees each week. When, for whatever reasons, churchgoers find themselves in disagreement with the pastor or the church's programs, they find ways to express that disagreement.

And one way is by writing a letter. One pastor's wife reported that she would not let her husband look at mail on his day off. Ed rarely opens mail for any reason, and I try to protect him from discouragement on his day off as well as on Sunday. But I often save mail I have opened for him if it contains criticism or issues that need to be dealt with at the church.

At a dinner with several couples, the subject of criticism became the topic. Ed and I stifled a laugh when one woman at the table expressed utter shock that people would write letters of criticism to a minister. The Holy Spirit had changed her life through Bible study and application. Even her marriage had been saved. In light of her experience, she could not imagine people would talk negatively about what the pastor said or did. Unfortunately, the more she associates with Christians the more she will find out.

Pastors can often guess which events will trigger people to write letters of complaint. Ed automatically thinks ahead about how to deal with the matter. When he "feels it comin'" he tells the congregation, "Don't bother writing about what I'm going to address!"

I have not met anyone in ministry who has not struggled with the negative letters they receive—wondering if they are written as constructive criticism or slander or something in between. Someone always has an idea about how things should or could have been done differently, and not all pastors exude approachability. If a person in the congregation feels worried about speaking to the pastor personally, he or she may put in writing a concern that could otherwise have been easily and quickly discussed. On the other hand, a pastor who is approachable is likely to receive even more letters. Such letters generally come in one of two forms: signed and anonymous.

Signed letters of criticism need to be handled with great care by pastors. Whether or not the letters are written in a loving spirit should not be the determinant for change. Some letters, written in a critical spirit, point out errors that deserve attention. Other letters, written in a constructive spirit, are not right in their demand for change. Pastors should read any signed, critical letters in the light of Scripture, determine whether they as ministers are in error biblically, and then respond to the writer.

People want to be heard, and sometimes they may come across in a letter as critical when really they only want to understand specific matters better. If the pastor's response is not defensive or argumentative, the writer may be satisfied with the information given. Chronic faultfinders and grumblers cannot be satisfied, however. Ed and I have gained enough wisdom through the years to help us know the difference between real concern and the desire simply to complain.

Before we move on to a discussion of anonymous letters, there is another method of expressing disagreement, closely allied with letter writing, that should be discussed. This method is one of the fastest ways to divide and split a church. It is the petition. If a pet issue is not handled by the pastor or the board within a perceived time frame, a complainant may resort to passing a petition. Petitions generally arise over matters that have not been considered with true spiritual maturity by the complainant. Moreover, petitions are often spearheaded by people whose desire is to control. They are the result of wanting to pick sawdust out of our brother's and sister's eyes when we have planks in our own (Matt. 7:3; Luke 6:41).

Jesus taught His disciples the basic principle in regard to judging, condemning, and forgiving. That this principle is found twice in Scripture indicates its importance. We must remind ourselves of sawdust and planks when we are tempted to complain. People who complain, judge, condemn, or are unforgiving *are* blind, yet they are trying to lead or change others whom they *perceive* to be blind. They cannot see spiritually because of their own sin, yet they concentrate their efforts on fixing the behavior of others.

In truth, most people have spiritual blind spots. When we are willing to give careful attention to our own blind spots as God's Word reveals them to us, we realize that petitioning for our pet issues in the church is not an appropriate way to change things, nor does it help reach people who need the Lord. Petitions do not communicate unity among our Christian brothers and sisters.

Anonymous letters are another way of addressing complaints to the pastor. I wonder how many people have wanted to change their names to Anonymous. Then they could write their pastor a letter, telling him in no uncertain terms what they think—no-holds-barred, no fear of judgment. Do angry writers seriously think that a pastor would change his thoughts or actions based solely on an anonymous letter?

For years Ed struggled over whether to read anonymous letters or throw them away. His dad advised him, many times, that they were not worth reading. Reading harsh words, even if unsigned, could bring on long bouts of introspection. Ed would wonder when he talked with people whether they were the writers, and if he would ever be able to resolve the issue. When Ed received a long, nasty, scathing letter signed "Saint," he was at last able to settle the matter. He told his secretary to throw away any anonymous mail.

A few unsigned letters have recently made their way to our home. I read the first one before throwing it away. Now, before reading a letter, I check for a signature. If there is not one it is relegated to the trash can. I have learned that beating the air is illogical and useless. It is better for me to pray that God will change my heart—or the writer's—rather than stew over unsigned complaints.

Another ineffective way to express disagreement with the pastor is passing on a complaint through the pastor's wife or family (see chap. 13). This method is particularly bad if it carries a threat of what will happen if action is not taken. A burden like that should never be laid on the pastor's spouse or family. The complaint should be addressed directly to the pastor or lay leadership and worked through the appropriate channels.

Criticism can tear down a pastor's spirit even though he's aware that everyone called by God will, at some time, face criticism. Like the prophet Elijah, a pastor may feel as if he has been rejected and is "the only one left," standing alone, "zealous for the LORD God Almighty." In Elijah's time God had reserved seven thousand others in Israel who followed Him (1 Kings 19:9–18). And in modern churches, many members of the body will stand with a pastor who preaches God's Truth.

## Chapter 16

# A BETTER WAY

In any communication with a pastor—whether by letter or in person—Christians should always tell the truth. Church members who need to communicate with their ministers about difficult circumstances should accurately describe all the issues and details pertinent to the situation. Not only will their own spiritual growth be impeded if they distort the truth, but eventually they will fall into their own trap (Prov. 28:10). It is very likely that dishonest people will be trying to use a pastor to enhance their spiritual growth.

Before writing a letter to the pastor, consider whether a person-to-person meeting would be better for discussing and resolving the issue. Speaking face-to-face with a person is probably the best method of communication, even if it requires traveling.

On the other hand, you may be able to say what you think more clearly on paper. And clear thinking is, of course, a major consideration when communicating with a pastor—especially when you are passionate about a matter. As long as the passion is not driven by anger, a letter is a perfectly good option. Sometimes a compromise between a letter and a face-to-face talk with the pastor may be helpful. When I am presenting a proposal or discussing a major concern, having the main points written and in front of me during the discussion helps me to remember what I want to say and to stick to my points. I have chosen this route sometimes when a letter I have already written seems to convey the wrong spirit.

If, after considering the above advice, you decide that writing to the pastor is the best option, your letter will be more effective if some important principles are kept in mind. The purpose of the letter should be to keep the doors of communication open, not to shut them. Although a letter may clarify or state issues, it will always be more likely to gain a hearing if it edifies the pastor rather than tears him down.

An older pastor once gave Ed some sage advice: "Be very careful what you put in writing, because it could come back to haunt you." Thus, if critical matters are lying heavily on your heart, you would be wise not to compose a letter in the heat of emotion. Asking yourself the following questions will help keep the letter in the right spirit:

1. Will this letter edify?
2. If the content is negative, is it necessary?
3. Is every bit of information in the letter truthful?
4. What state are my emotions in?
5. If the concern is not handled to my liking, am I prepared to follow biblical guidelines in taking it further?
6. Does my reaction to this matter demonstrate a desire for God's will or for my will?
7. What part should prayer play in composing the letter?

Before mailing the letter, it would be advisable to let a couple of friends read it first. Then let it lie for a day or two before mailing it or tossing it in the trash. Once the letter is mailed, it would be a good idea to give the pastor plenty of time to respond before following up with a call or second letter. Answering mail is not one of my husband's favorite activities, but he often calls a person in response to a letter, especially if the letter contains criticism. Ed feels that talking through an issue, once it has been raised, is better than writing another letter in response. A timely phone call can disarm a person ready for a paper fight. Often, when the letter writer hears Ed's voice on the phone and hears his perspective or explanation, the writer is considerably calmed. If, after discussion, there is still disagreement, Ed tries to end the conversation, agreeing to disagree or meet face-to-face for further discussion. Even a telephone call cannot be as fruitful as a personal meeting, since body language is often a better indicator of attitude than words are.

It is best to settle disagreement with the pastor according to the biblical outline. If a matter cannot be resolved in biblical order (directly with the person or in the company of several witnesses), then the church board should handle it. Within any church, a system will have been developed for settling concerns before the governing board. No one should ever make accusations about moral character without having two or more witnesses and without following the delineated church policy. If an accuser is unwilling to follow procedures, an issue can become a "shootin' match," and all parties involved are injured. Politicking within the church detracts from its mission and expends years of the minister's heart and energy. The ability to serve the Lord with joy is the first thing that the pastor loses.

When people experience problems with their pastor, they should ask themselves, "Is it a matter that can be handled through personal contact, or does the matter relate to the pastor's work in such a way that I should seek the godly counsel of the board chairman?" Even people not actively involved in church leadership can, through reading and study, become informed on matters of conflict resolution.[1] Accounts of the various issues that ministry leaders have faced may help lay and ministry people alike gain perspective on their own problems before unnecessarily causing more.

Timing, for instance, can be everything. "One ministry couple . . . was subjected to harsh criticism as they struggled with [serious family problems]. The elders of the church were aware of their pain, but chose that time to unload a series of complaints on the father. It was the proverbial straw that broke their backs: they resigned from that ministry and are currently in another profession."[2]

We all need to check our motives when discussing our "concerns" with those who minister to us. Whether we are dealing with matters of immorality or matters of preference, each situation needs to be handled with a heart that is listening to God for direction. Unity rather than division in the family of God should be the goal of each conflict resolution. The resolution of serious conflicts should not become occasions for gossip, especially in the name of prayer requests. Too often, the temptation to sensationalize does irreparable damage. If we follow the directives of our respective churches, we fall in line with a command that I have quoted twice before this, the very verse of Scripture, in fact, that the Lord used to prompt me to write this book—Hebrews 13:17:

> *Obey your leaders and submit to their authority. They keep watch over you as men who must give an account. Obey them so that their work will be a joy, not a burden, for that would be of no advantage to you.*

Let me offer one more caution about conflict resolution. No matter what your grievance and no matter how hard you try to resolve it, no matter how godly the church leadership or how gently a matter may be disputed, the end result may not be to your satisfaction. A former chairman of our elder board, a person I highly respect, told me that dissatisfaction often follows the resolution of disagreements, partly because emotions and expectations are raised, partly because communication is never perfect, and mostly because people are never perfect. Realizing that disagreements are inevitable between imperfect human beings helps us deal with imperfect results. It also helps us practice the gift of grace giving.

*Section 6*

# HONORING YOUR PASTOR

*Chapter 17*

# SHARING THE JOYS

Ed and I have been enriched by the many joys we have experienced in ministry. Although ministry life is sometimes difficult and frustrating, not every day is hard. I feel privileged to be the wife of a pastor. For as long as I can remember I have prayed to God that I would be thankful for everything He has given me—an abundance of spiritual, physical, and material gifts of every kind. During the hours I have spent remembering and writing about these blessings for this book, I have felt renewed joy and gratitude. It is with that feeling that I write this chapter.

Several references appear in Scripture with regard to apostles receiving honor (Acts 28:10), and elders, whose lives and work, "preaching and teaching" in the church are worthy (1 Tim. 5:17), receiving double honor (Greek meaning is double pay). Some churches today seem to have little idea of what double pay means. Ministry people report eking out an existence on a salary that barely covers the minimum necessities. Scripture also says that it is right for the minister to receive wages for his labor (1 Cor. 9:5–14; 1 Tim. 5:18). *The Living Bible* states that "pastors who do their work well should be paid well and should be highly appreciated, especially those who work hard at both preaching and teaching." (1 Tim. 5:17) Yet pastors often feel that their pay is grudgingly given by church members, some of whom could afford to give much more. Providing the pastor and his family with what they need to live is the church's responsibility, just as it is the pastor's responsibility to provide ministry to the church. Each blesses the other. But this chapter is about much more than money or salary. It is about becoming a source of encouragement to our pastors, which is in part giving them due honor. It is about giving from the heart.

The primary gift we can give our pastors is to be kind to one another—to avoid judging and criticizing each other. When I was young, I was taught to hate what was evil (Rom. 12:9), but I often took that teaching too far. I thought that when Christian brothers and sisters did something I was unfamiliar with or that conflicted with my preferences, they were to be avoided. I feared contaminating my personal interpretation of Christian living. Whether or not the objects of my displeasure actually practiced sinful behavior, I questioned their motives and spiritual depth. I was afraid to judge ministers, however, because I feared God's judgment on me. Yet I wondered how a minister could be right if I was right. As I have grown more mature in the Lord, I have come to believe that we as Christians will be in for a surprise when we get to heaven and see who is there. I wonder how much fellowship we miss by being so judgmental.

Sometimes we do not reserve our judgment only for those who we perceive as sinful or those who are going through bad times; many Christians have a difficult time uplifting one another during times that are especially *good*. We seem to be able to "mourn with those who mourn," but struggle to "rejoice with those who rejoice" (Rom. 12:15). It is easier to fall into criticizing, judging, condemning, and questioning motives and worthiness. True, we do not deserve good through our own merit. It is always with thanks to the grace of God that we are able to enjoy abundant life in Him. But when good comes along in the life of a brother or sister, we need to express joy for him or her.

We do not need to tear down a person's spirit "lest he become proud." God takes care of the humbling process without our help. And neither are pastors spared from being kept in check by their congregations. Whatever they say or do seems to become fair game.

Romans chapter 12 gives us insight into specific ways that Christians should relate to one another. The commands in this chapter are powerful. But in applying the principles outlined in there, Christians are often guilty of disobedience. We often display animosity. Romans 12 begins by outlining the principles behind our relationship with God: we must offer our bodies as living sacrifices; cease to conform to worldly patterns; be transformed by the renewing of our minds; be tested by doing God's good, pleasing, and perfect will. Then comes the nitty-gritty: "Do not think of yourself more highly than you ought" (v. 3). Ed says it in everyday language, "Don't lie to yourself."

Every phrase in Romans 12 deserves meditation, but when it comes to the way Christian laypeople and their ministers relate to one another, verse 10 has long haunted me: "Be devoted to one another in brotherly love. Honor one another above yourselves."

It is good when young people, as a result of being taught to set high standards for their lives, place great value on doing what is right according to God's Word. Some Christians, however—whether by example or by their own interpretation of Scripture—become proud and judgmental of others who live, worship, or look differently from themselves. The teaching for living "in harmony" (v. 16) with Christians is either ignored or disobeyed—certainly not lived out. This was the way I was in my youth. But because of my husband's love for all people, my path crossed with those of Christians from all kinds of backgrounds. I began to open my heart to sincere brotherly love. Through that growth, I also began to recognize the enemy more clearly and learn more about my responsibility to my brothers and sisters in Christ. We must honor others above ourselves. This principle can easily be forgotten when personalities and preferences are given precedence, or when concepts are exalted, far above their own worth, to the status of absolute truth.

Church members who separate clear scriptural teaching from personal or cultural preferences display spiritual maturity. The ability to make such distinctions enables believers to become devoted to and give honor to Christians whose comfort zone, living patterns, and worship may not be the same as their own. Relationships in the family of God are always more important than personal preferences.

Fortunately, prejudice and self-righteousness do not prevail in every church, although it is likely that any church can experience a degree of either of them at some time. Thus, I encourage all Christians to practice the biblical directives for brotherly devotion. By doing so, we can become a source of encouragement to our pastors—which is a part of giving them due honor.

Consider the case of Marlene Reuben. Ed and Marlene's husband, Spencer, were so much alike they became soul brothers. They even looked alike and wore the same size clothing. Several months after Spencer was killed in an automobile crash, Marlene presented Ed with Spencer's stylish wardrobe. It so happened that Ed was in desperate need of new clothing at that time. Ed's thank you to Marlene was that he would pray for her when he put on Spencer's clothes. But because of this tragedy Ed received another gift that he highly values. Out of her grief, Marlene began a ministry to widows in our church. Because of God's call and blessing, her ministry has developed far beyond anything that a committee or staff member could have conceived. Seeing church members minister to their Christian brothers and sisters is a wonderful gift to a pastor, one that enables the pastor to serve with joy.

We are thankful that few gifts are the result of grief. An indescribable bonding occurs when a pastor becomes involved with families through the death of a loved one. At such times gifts in the form of material goods are the last things on the minds of pastors. Ed has always felt that his involvement with families during their time of grief is one of the most important avenues of ministry he has. He decided as a very young pastor that because funerals are part of what he is called to do, he would not accept money. Many pastors will, however, accept monetary payment through the funeral director because the pastor and his family need it.

There is grave danger in ministry persons expecting special payments, discounts, favors, recognition, or bonuses. Grand Rapids, Michigan, has nearly five hundred Protestant churches and many more non-Protestant ones, accounting for thousands of ministry people. Some of them demand a "minister's discount" at retail stores. Chuck Swindoll has addressed the subject of materialistic temptations on his radio program. He warns people in ministry to live their lives as examples, "not (lovers) of money"(1 Tim. 3:3); "not pursuing dishonest gain" (Titus 1:7); "not greedy for money" (1 Peter 5:2). "Yes," Chuck states, "it was a struggle when I had less than I have now." But as Chuck reminds us, whatever our economic level, we must all guard against the temptation to love money. The battle to resist materialism may be complicated when we accept unsolicited gifts and favors; we may desire more when we are given more.

The American dream is to earn enough money for life to be easier than when we were children and to be able to set enough aside for retirement to be easier still. But if that dream were to come true for everyone, no one could ever be conformed to the image of Christ. God's plan for our spiritual growth does not involve money. And, of course, money is no guarantee against problems. The tabloids would go out of business if millionaires had no problems. In the ministry, we learn about giving of ourselves, and we also need to place proper priority on receiving. In many ways, however, ministry has more benefits or perks than any other profession. Those benefits come to us spiritually through our own developing relationship with the Lord, through our service, and through the fruitful lives of believers. Gifts to a pastor certainly do not need to come in a material form.[1] Believers can uplift their pastor, perhaps at a time when he most needs it, simply by telling him of their spiritual growth. The life of a growing, faithful Christian is an encouragement to a minister. It would be a welcome gift if churchgoers shared with their pastor specific ways that the Lord is working in their lives through the pastor's ministry.

A woman waited in a reception line after church for over an hour after a surprise tenth anniversary celebration for Ed and me. She told Ed with great joy how much she had grown spiritually from his recent four-week series on stewardship, and she wanted to thank him.

That kind of sharing is much more satisfying and lasting than earthly gifts. Not only does the pastor have responsibilities to the congregation because of his calling, but also the congregation has a responsibility to express more than "lofty expectations" and criticism. The "greatness [of a church] is demonstrated by the love the people in a congregation have for each other and for those God positions at their head as ministers."[2]

After I fell on ice about ten years ago, I suffered hand and arm pain. Now, after several years of God's grace and healing—as well as medical treatment and physical and nutritional therapy—the pain has subsided. But for a period of time it was difficult for me to perform everyday functions, especially playing the piano for our church choir. One woman, who was particularly sensitive to my condition, paid her cleaning lady to clean my house during the time of our ten Christmas programs and again during our Easter celebration programs. The giver of that gift holds a special place in my heart! (One of my neighbors, who does not go to our church, also helped me several times free of charge, even though cleaning homes was her job.) After I recovered, I cleaned a friend's home while she was ill. It was a gift to her, but also it was a kind of thank offering to God for all the people who had helped me.

Nonmaterial gifts that benefit the pastor's children are also a blessing. Nothing delights the hearts of parents more than someone taking a genuine interest in their children. Friends have taught our children how to fish, plant trees, mend fences, create school or AWANA projects, and do simple carpentry. Many gifts have been in the form of recreation—downhill, cross-country, or water skiing and paint-ball wars, to name a few. Senior high sponsors have spent immeasurable time with our children, fostering their spiritual development through Bible study and sharing personal time doing things the kids enjoy, especially hanging out in their homes making chocolate chip cookies.

With genuine love and a little creative thinking, church members can find ways to show their appreciation to their pastors. These gifts from the heart encourage a pastor to serve with enthusiasm and with joy.

*Chapter 18*

# SHARING THE WEALTH

A friend said to me, "Haven't you had enough given to you already? You're writing a book to get more gifts?" My answer is a resounding—No! Our family has been given so much, and we are deeply grateful. But some ministry people rarely receive gifts. And after reading the last chapter, which encouraged giving pastors gifts from the heart, readers may wince at the thought of giving more than they already give. And giving something extra to your pastor or the pastor's family is not even on the list. The ideas in this chapter are not for the purpose of asking you to give. They are merely suggestions for those who are able, and who want to express their feelings and demonstrate their love.

No one can give to everyone in every situation every time. I, too, struggle with gift giving. As a pastor's wife, I receive myriad invitations to baby and bridal showers, weddings and anniversaries, graduation, retirement, and birthday parties. It is difficult to set boundaries. It was difficult when we began a church in a little mountain town in Virginia, and it is difficult today in our church of thousands.

One thing I know for sure, though—a pastor and his family cannot live exemplary Christian lives if they are only on the receiving end of gifts. I would never want people to think that we were not appreciative or that we could ever take receiving gifts for granted. We must all express thanks. We must develop hearts of gratitude that will be passed on to our children and give the Lord the glory for the abundance of gifts He showers on us.

The discussion in this chapter relates to gifts given by lay-people out of gratitude and love to those who minister to them. But not every congregation gives gifts that build up the pastor and his spouse. I know of a church board that gave its pastor and his wife a meat platter every year. In that parish, individuals rarely uttered a word of affirmation or appreciation. The pastor and his wife often wondered if their efforts were worth expending. Even if that church community had been economically poor, a word of love and encouragement would have had more value than a tiffany lamp to the pastor and his wife. One wonders if anyone in the congregation or on the governing board had even thought about what they gave their minister. Perhaps the meat platter was not meant as a token, but it could easily be perceived as such. Gifts given under a spirit of obligation can dishearten even the most dedicated servants.

Churches vary considerably in their cultures and traditions. Many do not give the pastor a gift for Christmas at all; some give a monetary bonus. Our church does not give bonuses and only in recent years has given Christmas gifts to the pastoral or lay-staff, although we have been blessed by gifts on special occasions. At those times, it has been obvious that people have put a lot of thought into the gifts. They wanted to give us something that would be meaningful.

Church members who would like to do something "different" for their minister might consider doing a little detective work . . . like the friend who just called me.

"Does pastor have a laptop computer?" the caller asked. "Well, yes, he does, but he doesn't use it very often. He's more comfortable writing longhand on a legal pad," I replied. The caller said, "We were thinking of giving him a lap desk as a thank you for being our pastor. We found that we use our laptop much more with a lap desk for it on our favorite chair." A few weeks later, they delivered the gift to our front door. Ed does use his computer on it and is very grateful!

Knowing a pastor's background, interests, and hobbies is a help when church members feel moved to buy a gift for their pastor. It would be wise, though, to find out if your pastor already has all the theme gifts he can use. My husband is Irish and played soccer until he blew out his knee two years ago, so he receives gifts related to his home country, his culture, and his favorite sport. We have been given beautiful photograph books of Ireland that I display on shelves and tables. We have also been given gorgeous Waterford crystal and Belleek china that we use and enjoy. Then, just for fun, people have given Ed leprechaun shoe and dolls, mugs with Irish jokes on them, flags of Ireland, and many items adorned with shamrocks.

One woman, who had already given lovely gifts of remembrance to each of us, called to ask me if Ed had a clock with a soccer ball on it. I thanked her for her thoughtfulness, but said we already had more clocks than we could use. I suggested that Ed would be grateful if she donated to a missionary cause instead.

We have been truly blessed by the generosity of people. Over the years Ed, the children, and I have received many gifts. Some of these thoughtful ideas may inspire readers who are thinking about presenting their pastors with something. We have received gifts in the form of waived medical and other professional fees, house and yard maintenance, magazine subscriptions, flowers, restaurant and book gift certificates, golf lessons and equipment for the game, and several vehicles. At times, these gifts were necessities that arrived just when we needed them most.

Whether or not gifts are in answer to a prayer, all items received are considered gifts from God. Most have been treats that people have given to us either as an expression of thanks for our ministry or in response to a particular situation. For example, one family gave a detailed car cleaning to us because we had loaned them a car in their time of need.

For my fortieth birthday, one of my first friends in the church invited a group of women to her home for a party. It was a wonderful way for me to meet with them all, and their generosity was overwhelming. Some gifts I received that day were unique, such as gift certificates for a facial or a manicure. The happy memory of how pampered I felt has inspired me to give the same sort of gifts to others.

I am grateful for the love people have demonstrated through gifts, but I am also reminded that Ed and I, too, have an obligation to others. While we may not have always been able to offer expensive gifts, we have followed through with a commitment we made over twenty-five years ago to give generously, sometimes sacrificially, to others. When Ed and I heard a message early in our marriage on biblical giving, we realized that we should do more than merely tithe. We felt that we should also give sacrificially, by faith. We started by giving fuel oil to a couple who could not afford to fill the tank of their huge old home. Living on a small budget, we had no idea how we would pay the bill ourselves, but we called the oil company anyway. Before the bill arrived, Ed received a check for some work he had done but had not expected payment for. We were delighted and felt that God's provision was an encouragement for us to do more for others in need. Likewise, we have no idea how many gifts have been given to us that were sacrificial on the givers' part. It is a matter that is and should be between each giver and God.

Even though we, as Christians, are not to give with the motive of receiving, God often does provide gifts in return, which should prod us to do even more for others. The principle for giving is stated in Luke 6:38: "Give, and it will be given to you. A good measure, pressed down, shaken together and running over, will be poured into your lap. For with the measure you use, it will be measured to you." The bigger the measuring cup, the bigger the blessing.[1]

Another creative gift idea might be offering the pastor and his family a retreat. We usually try to plan family vacations within our budget, but we have sometimes been invited to use other people's cottages. We also have been provided with weekends away—sometimes just for Ed and me, and sometimes for the whole family. In 1991, our family enjoyed a one-month vacation in Northern Ireland through the generosity of some of our members who wanted their pastor to visit his homeland. An aunt and uncle allowed us for three weeks to use their apartment overlooking the ocean. We had not been there for thirteen years, and our children were old enough to remember many relatives and special places.

Then in March 1997, to celebrate our tenth anniversary of pastoring at Calvary, the church surprised Ed and me with tickets to Belfast. Thinking that this might be the last major trip we could take with the children as "children," we went as a family. We all have wonderful memories of the country and of many cousins and aunts and uncles, their favorite coffee shop and restaurant—Morelli's!—and many ancient historical attractions. After three weeks of riding together in a "wee" car (generously loaned by an aunt), running through subway corridors, sleeping in small quarters, and sharing a bathroom, we were delighted to discover that we actually liked being together! It was fun, and I felt a twinge of sadness as we came home to a parting of the ways in four different cars. We are deeply thankful for the generosity of our Christian family.

Ed and I attended a caregiving retreat designed to renew ministry couples (another creative gift idea for a pastor and spouse). The retreat was developed by laypeople with a burden to encourage God's servants. A couple whom we met there invited us to share an elegant meal in a baseball stadium restaurant during a game. The tickets and meal were provided by a businessman in their church who encourages them to share his gift with other people in ministry. Ed and I were grateful to this person, a person we never met, who has a heart for sharing his wealth with people in ministry. The dinner and game were a material perk, but the occasion also did a lot for us emotionally. It strengthened our kinship with another ministry couple with whom we have a lot in common. Without such a gift, we might have only talked for years about "getting together." Now, every time we drive past that stadium in Chicago, we remember the couple with fondness and the businessman with gratitude.

A gift that helped us focus on issues in ministry, as a couple, was a year's subscription to Pastor-to-Pastor tapes, produced by Focus on the Family. When we received each set of tapes every other month, we listened to them separately and together, usually in the car. The tapes gave us insight into the challenges we had already faced and into ones we probably will face. We enjoyed many interesting discussions because of them. A church's budget may allow for these resources for the pastor, but he may not be aware of the tape series. If readers are interested in providing the tapes as a gift, they could ask the pastor or his secretary whether he is already receiving the tapes. They can easily be ordered and sent directly to the pastor's home.

Some people have a favorite magazine such as *Guideposts* or *Israel, My Glory* and think it would be nice for the pastor and his family to enjoy it as well. Publications given as gifts have been a blessing, educationally and spiritually. Many pastors already receive magazines such as *Leadership Journal* or *Biblical Archeology.* An interested church member could simply ask if the pastor has a preference for a particular publication.

Many pastors' wives enjoy reading about ministry from their peers' perspectives, but they report that subscriptions are a low priority in their budget. Since pastors' wives are usually not on church staff, no money is allocated for ministry-related resources, retreats, or conferences for them the way it probably is for their husbands. The following nondenominational publication would be an excellent idea for anyone wishing to take out a subscription for their pastor's wife.

*Just Between Us* is a quarterly magazine for women in ministry, edited by Jill Briscoe. Topics include personal spiritual growth, forced termination, the challenges missionary wives face in changing cultures every term and furlough, and much more. Call 1-800-260-3342 for current subscription information.

If ordering a magazine subscription for the pastor's wife is not in your budget either, many pastor's wives would consider it a wonderful gift to know about the following free Web site tailored specifically to meet their needs.

*The Pastor's Wife* is edited monthly by Janice Hildreth and is available only on-line. One monthly feature is a question submitted by a pastor's wife (subscriber) concerning a situation she is facing. Subscribers are invited to respond with advice, and a sampling of the answers is printed. For subscription information log on to www.pastorswife.com.

Gift giving to pastors varies in the different church cultures. Growing up in South Carolina and later living as an adult in Virginia, I noticed a difference between African-American pastors and some white pastors. Even in the poor black communities, many of the pastors drive an expensive car and dress in the finest clothes. On the other hand, many pastors of lower or middle class white churches dress very modestly and drive average cars. They may not want to spend more money on a car or on clothes than appears reasonable to the congregation.

The practices of African-American churches date back many years to times when their pastors were the only people with freedom, prestige, and standing in their communities. The members of African-American churches lavished gifts, money, and fine meals on their pastors in order to uphold that status. It is thought that African-American churchgoers lived vicariously through their pastors, giving their pastors the lives they themselves could never attain. In some communities the practice still exists. On a special day, churchgoers bring money to the church to fill a money tree or place their gifts in the offering plate to show their love to the pastor.

Dolphus Weary, for many years, headed the Mendenhall Ministries in Mendenhall, Mississippi. As a poor black child in rural Mississippi, Dolphus learned "that no matter how little you have, you still have a responsibility toward someone somewhere—in the church, or in the community—who has less than you have." He understood that principle but wrestled for a long time with the matter of giving to the pastor so that he could live extravagantly. Weary's heartfelt desire was for someone to "turn this thing around" and see more given to the poor than to the preacher who already had more than anyone else did![2] When Weary left home to get an education, his intention was to never return to the place he had left or to its way of life. Through God's guidance, however, he was called to help educate, train, and give hope to his own community. He did so for many years, living modestly among those to whom he ministered.

Whether or not a church and its members lavish material support on a pastor, it is important that Christians give the respect and honor due a pastor. The way in which respect and honor are demonstrated may be material or spiritual and will always be subject to culture and custom. If material, it is considered above and beyond tithing, which is giving to the Lord and His work as an act of obedience. Remember that Jesus praised the widow who gave all she had, not the rich people who threw in large amounts of money out of their wealth (Mark 12:41–44). And remember, too—no matter what their financial status, the best and most important gift church members can give is time spent praying for the pastors and church leaders. We all can pray at any time, anywhere, and without cost.

*Section 7*

# LETTING GO OF YOUR PASTOR

*Chapter 19*

# OPEN THE DOOR WITH GRACE AND SAY GOOD-BYE

Bill and Barb had pastored a church for nearly twenty years. They were very sad to leave the people in that congregation; they loved them like family. The church was generous in their send-off, both emotionally and spiritually, understanding Bill's call to a new ministry in a different town. The struggle that followed, however, was complex. Even though Barb knew they had made the right move, she missed the attention she had received as the pastor's wife in her old church. Because she felt a personal call to ministry, she began to know, love, and witness to her new neighbors and get involved in another local church. Still, she missed her old friends.

Then the struggle became more difficult. The new pastor settled into Bill's old church, but some of the members wanted Bill to perform weddings for their children. After all, they had grown up with his children. It was at this time that Bill and Barb had to make it clear to their friends and to the church board that they did not want to cause any division in the church or hard feelings with the new pastor. They had to stay away for a long time before they could even visit. Now, more than a decade later, they still maintain deep friendships with a few people from that church, but they spend time with them in another state.

The members in Bill and Barb's old church had a wonderful relationship with their former pastor, but it created a touchy situation when they looked to Bill for advice after he had left. Likewise, Bill could not continue his old friendships on the same level as when he pastored the old church. Bill's old church had looked to him for godly leadership and wisdom when he was their pastor. Bill continued to show this godly leadership and wisdom in refusing to become involved in any current controversies in his old church. If the new pastor decided to look to the former pastor for counsel, their friendship could have developed. This would have been a bonus for the members. I have seldom, though, heard of this happening.

Many pastors' wives report that it would have been better for them and their husbands if the former pastors of their churches had not stayed in the community when they retired. A former pastor seems to have an aura of authority, whether he intends to or not, and people have a difficult time switching their allegiance to a new leader as long as he is around. Although church members usually have no control over whether a retiring pastor remains, they would be wise to respect the perspective of the new pastor. Even in the best of situations, a new leader needs several years to feel settled and comfortable.

If the new pastor constantly hears how "dear Former Pastor So-and-So" did things, he will have difficulty feeling that the congregation is willing to give him the freedom to shepherd the flock his own way. No minister can be like his predecessor, even if the new person was trained by or worked as an intern or associate for many years under the retired pastor. It is unrealistic for a congregation to expect a new pastor to maintain the status quo. But many preachers have been driven away because the congregation balked at change or because the retired pastor actually undermined the position of his replacement. Resistance to change and to the new pastor can occur even when the former pastor was forced to leave a pastorate.

And some pastors contribute to their own difficulty. We have known pastors who went into churches with a plan to change things, and when this plan was implemented too soon, confusion and dissension were the outcome—and "out came" the pastor! Rather than charging in like a bull, the new pastor needs to take time, learn as much as possible about the new situation, and give time for personalities, styles, and attitudes to surface.

Retiring pastors may face a dilemma if their children have grown up and are settled into the old community. Naturally, the family benefits if they can live in close proximity. But if they choose to do this, they should be sensitive to the new pastor and his struggle to become oriented to the church—especially if the retiring couple continues to attend the church. Their old church has been home, and it is not easy for them to leave the church and people they love and start worshiping and making new friends in a different church. The retiring couple still needs the loving prayers of the congregation.

Some pastors experience "forced termination." It may shock you to learn that "ministers are being terminated at the alarming rate of hundreds per month."[1] Church members who want to get rid of their pastor for personal reasons may be too immature spiritually to search their hearts and Scripture for a solution to the situation. Even when a church's problems can only be resolved by the resignation of the pastor, members should have the courtesy to treat the departing pastor and his family with fairness and dignity.

We have known many brothers and sisters in Christ who have slaughtered one another verbally and emotionally. As one Christian psychotherapist stated, "Churches are systemic organizations. They may be ordained of God, but they are governed and administered by human beings."[2] Sometimes it is the ministers who are to blame. They deify their own preferences or credit

God with authorizing whatever they personally think is right.[3] In situations of forced termination, it is often difficult to know who to blame. It becomes all the more important to follow biblical principles—to refrain from gossip and to remember that we are commanded to love one another.

Church members who are not part of the governing process can best help by abstaining from ill will and words. And by praying. Everyone can pray about the hurt, grief, embarrassment, isolation, and fear that the departing family is experiencing. It is unfortunate that some people pray more often for God's judgment than for reconciliation or guidance. If a pastor is asked to leave because some immorality has been revealed and is being dealt with, that is cause for rejoicing—not rejoicing over the catastrophe that follows the revelation of the sin, but rejoicing that the sinful behavior is no longer hidden. Secret sins produce an unhealthy spiritual community. Ed and I have shed many tears over ministry friends who have left their churches under a shadow. I have asked God for the grace to remember that we need to be on our guard so that we do not fall in the same way.

If, however, a pastor is forced to leave over matters of preference rather than theological or immoral consideration, hurt feelings are likely to remain unresolved in the congregation and, sometimes, within the minister's family. Often the children of pastors will eventually walk away from any appearance of religion if their disappointment and grief is not processed biblically.

When a church board feels it is necessary to terminate a pastor, all church members, whether or not they understand the intricacies of the situation, are obligated to pray for and follow their board's leadership. When one pastor was asked to resign, people called the church office for more information. The church secretary said, tactfully, "Trust the council's leadership and pray for them." Those who force the termination of people called to minister to them will be held accountable before God, just as the ministry people will be held accountable. When the board functions with unity, they serve a purpose: no one handles matters alone and no one person takes the brunt of criticism. At the same time, we are all responsible for our own actions, behaviors, and thoughts, whether we are misguided by spiritually immature leadership or are ourselves part of the decision-making processes in church government.

In denominations that have a superintendent or governing body that appoints ministers to congregations, the laypeople may not be aware of the steps in the process or what a pastor does to prepare himself and his family to leave one church and go to another. By purposely educating themselves about the way their church "passes the mantle," church members may not only positively affect their own attitudes and perspectives about the outgoing and incoming ministers but also help other church members adjust as well.

Change is difficult emotionally, physically, and spiritually. I admire people who stay with a church through its difficult times, particularly when a pastor is forced to leave, and the process of finding a new one is lengthy. Years ago, a pastor left a church a few miles from our own. The church sought Ed's counsel in the interim. Ed told the members of that church that while our resources were available to them for help during their difficult time, he did not want them at our church! He jokingly told them that we already had a parking problem, but more importantly, they needed to support each other as they searched for a new pastor. Many members appreciated hearing that comment, and it helped them decide not to float from church to church.

In some situations, it may be best to leave a church during transition. When I was a teenager, a pastor left my church. My mother felt that too much was being said publicly, things that young people should not hear. Accusations were being made about the pastor that should have been presented to the board behind closed doors. Judgments were shouted from people in the pews. The division was such that, rather than take sides,

Mother felt it best that we go to another church. Several years later, we returned to the first church and remained there until I was married and moved away. Now, as a mother, I appreciate her taking us out of that unhealthy situation. To this day, I do not know if the truth of the matter was ever revealed and handled properly.

When people return to churches after leaving during a stressful time—as my mother and my sisters and I did—those who have stayed and stuck it out may exhibit hard feelings. I do not remember people having ill will toward my family when we returned. As a pastor's wife, however, I have heard many people discuss their feelings about members who left and returned. Whether leaving and then returning is right or wrong cannot be settled here. The decisions people make are based on many factors, and sometimes others cannot appreciate their particular perspectives, especially in situations when emotions are close to the surface.

When the pastor leaves, hurt and frustration are common among church members. Sometimes, they are not able to come to some kind of closure in their relationships with the pastor, either because they were not part of the process of termination, or because they misunderstood their personal connection with him. It may even be that the situation was mishandled, and everyone is hurt. Many misunderstandings in churches result from lack of information, from preconceived or misconstrued expectations, and from a failure to observe clear scriptural directives. In chapter 2 of Paul's letter to the Philippians, we read:

> *Does it mean anything to you that we are brothers in the Lord, sharing the same Spirit? Are your hearts tender and sympathetic at all? Then make me truly happy by loving each other and agreeing wholeheartedly with each other, working together with one heart and mind and purpose.*

*Don't be selfish; don't live to make a good impression on others. Be humble, thinking of others as better than yourself. Don't just think about your own affairs, but be interested in others, too, and in what they are doing.*

*Your attitude should be the kind that was shown us by Jesus Christ, who, though he was God, did not demand and cling to his rights as God, but laid aside his mighty power and glory, taking the disguise of a slave and becoming like men. And he humbled himself even further, going so far as actually to die a criminal's death on a cross.*

*—Philippians 2:1–8* LB

If these principles were lived out in our churches, a significant amount of sin-based, proud, and selfish warfare would be avoided. As a result, it is quite likely that the number of pastoral terminations would be reduced. May God help each of us to practice Christ's attitude of undemanding humility. More than anything else, this Christlikeness—the evidence of spiritual maturity—will benefit the church during transition. The more people demonstrate godly attitudes, no matter how difficult the situation, the more a church can experience full unity to the glory of God.

*Section 8*

---

# EMPOWERING YOUR PASTOR
# TO SERVE WITH JOY

## *Chapter 20*

# THE FINAL CHALLENGE

All brothers and sisters in Christ have biblical responsibilities to one another. A list of those responsibilities can be found in 1 Thessalonians 5:12–25. They appear below so that each of us can check and double-check our own hearts, minds, and souls.

## Responsibilities Toward Ministers

- Respect those who work hard among you, who are over you, and who admonish you.
- Hold them in the highest regard in love because of their work.
- Live in peace with each other.

## Responsibility Toward Everyone

- Warn the idle, encourage the timid, help the weak, and be patient with everyone.
- Make sure that you do not pay back wrong with wrong, but always try to be kind to one another and to everyone else.

## Responsibility from Within Our Souls

- Be joyful always.
- Pray continually.
- Give thanks in all circumstances, for this is God's will for you in Christ Jesus.
- Do not put out the Spirit's fire.
- Do not treat prophecies with contempt.
- Test everything.
- Hold on to the good.
- Avoid every kind of evil.

## Our Promise and Hope

- The One who calls you is faithful and He will do it.

The last and most significant challenge I can leave with you is this: Brothers and sisters, pray for those who minister to you. It is the first and most important thing believers can do for their pastors and their pastors' families. The results are, of course, ultimately in God's hands, and the answers often unknown to those who pray. But when we go to God in prayer we have this assurance: "And I am sure that God who began the good work within you will keep right on helping you grow in his grace until his task within you is finally finished on that day when Jesus Christ returns" (Phil. 1:6 LB).

May we all experience growth in grace and joy—in service to Him.

# NOTES

## Chapter 3: What the Pastor Is Not

1. Name Withheld, "Loving the Unlovely," *Just Between Us,* spring 1997, 20.

2. John Ronsvalle and Sylvia Ronsvalle, *Beyond the Stained Glass Windows: Money Dynamics in the Church* (Grand Rapids: Baker, 1996), 57–58.

3. Lorna Dobson, *I'm More Than the Pastor's Wife* (Grand Rapids: Zondervan, 1995), 105.

4. Cheryl M. Smith, about Dr. Gloria Halverson, "Faith in Practice," *Just Between Us,* spring 1997, 8.

5. Ibid.

## Chapter 4: The Less-than-Private Lives of Pastors and Their Families

1. Lynne Dugan, ed., *Heart to Heart with Pastors' Wives* (Ventura, Calif.: Regal Books, 1994), 140.

2. H. B. London and Neil B. Wiseman, *Married to a Pastor's Wife* (Wheaton, Ill.: Victor, 1995), 167–68.

3.  Ideas taken from Karen Orfitelli, "How Much Should PKs Know About the Church?" *Pastor's Family,* August–September 1997, 26–28.

4.  Cameron Lee and Jack Balswick, *Life in a Glass House: The Minister's Family in Its Unique Social Context* (Grand Rapids: Zondervan, 1989), 175.

5.  Janice Hildreth, *The Pastor's Wife: An Interdenominational Newsletter for Women Married to Ministers* 4, no. 8 (August 1997).

## Chapter 5: Help for the Journey

1.  H. B. London Jr. and Neil B. Wiseman, *Married to a Pastor's Wife* (Wheaton, Ill.: Victor, 1995), 269.

## Chapter 6: R-E-S-P-E-C-T

1.  Ralph G. Turnbull, *A Minister's Obstacles* (Westwood, N.J.: Revell, 1996), 47.

2.  Jerry Falwell, ed., *Liberty Bible Commentary* (Nashville: Nelson, 1983; Lynchburg, Va.: Old Time Gospel Hour, 1983), 2: 581.

3.  Ray C. Stedman, with James C. Denney, *Adventuring Through the Bible: A Comprehensive Guide to the Entire Bible* (Grand Rapids: Discovery House, 1997), 647.

4.  Ibid., 59.

5.  Herbert Lockyer Sr., ed., *The Liberty Illustrated Bible Dictionary* (Nashville: Nelson, 1986), 488.

## Chapter 7: A Spring in the Desert

1.  Becky Beane, "My Kid's in Prison," *Jubilee,* spring 1997; idem, "Balm for the Wounded," *Jubilee,* spring 1997; idem, "Battered in Christ's Name," with sidebar by Rev. David Oyler, *Jubilee,* winter 1997; and idem, "The Crime the Church Can't Sweep Aside," *Jubilee,* winter 1997.

## Chapter 8: The Spring that Never Dries Up

1.  Wayne Jacobsen, "Seven Reasons for Staff Conflict," in *Leading Your Church Through Conflict and Reconciliation,* ed. Marshall Shelley (Minneapolis: Bethany House, 1997).

2.  Bill and Pam Farrel, "Protecting Your Relationship with Trust," in *Marriage in the Whirlwind: Seven Skills for Couples Who Can't Slow Down* (Downers Grove, Ill.: InterVarsity, 1996), 163–72.

3.  Heide Husted, "Four Ways I've Found Encouragement: Confessions of a Pastor Who Nearly Burned Out," *Leadership Journal,* summer 1996, 44.

4.  Judson Cornwall, *Praying the Scriptures: Communicating with God in His Own Words* (Lake Mary, Fla.: Creation House, 1988), 88.

5.  Andrew Murray, "The Spirit in Preacher and Hearer," in *God's Best Kept Secrets* (Grand Rapids: Kregel, 1995), 316.

## Chapter 9: Aid for Weary Travelers

1.  Yvonne Jones, preface to "Unpacking Your Emotional Bags," *Pastor's Family,* August–September 1997, 19.

2. Verdell Davis, *Let Me Grieve, but Not Forever* (Dallas: Word, 1994). This book was formerly titled *Riches Stored in Secret Places*. This is the best book I have read for dealing with grief and loss of all kinds. It is much more than the tragic story of Verdell's loss of her husband.

3. Paul F. Ford, *Companion to Narnia* (San Francisco: Harper, 1980), 333.

## Chapter 10: Mail Call

1. For specific examples of letters to clergy, useful for many occasions, see Guidepost's *The Someone Cares Encyclopedia of Letter Writing,* 1995.

## Chapter 11: Meal Call

1. Need some inspiration for hospitality? Read Rachael Crabb, *The Personal Touch: Encouraging Others Through Hospitality* (Colorado Springs: NavPress, 1990).

## Chapter 12: Motive, Timing, and Godless Chatter

1. Paul Meier, Frank Minirth et al., *What They Didn't Teach You in Seminary* (Nashville: Nelson, 1993), 277.

2. Jack Dunigan, "Cold Water," *Effective Leadership, A Bi-Monthly Resource of Ideas That Work for Leaders* 3, no. 4 (October 1997): 1.

## Chapter 13: Talking Face-to-Face with Your Pastor

1. Howard G. Hendricks and William D. Hendricks, *Living by the Book* (Chicago: Moody, 1991), 292.

2. Jill Briscoe, "Let Me Be David," part of a special section, "Being a Ministry Kid: Privilege or Punishment," *Just Between Us,* fall 1995, 14.

## Chapter 15: Not the Best Way

1. Philip Yancey, *What's So Amazing About Grace?* (Grand Rapids: Zondervan, 1997), 40.

## Chapter 16: A Better Way

1. Marshall Shelley, ed., *Leading Your Church Through Conflict and Reconciliation: Thirty Strategies to Transform Your Ministry,* Library of Leadership Development by Leadership/Christianity Today (Minneapolis: Bethany House, 1997). Chapters written by many pastors and ministry leaders.

2. David and Carolyn Roper, "When People Throw Stones," *Pastor's Family,* April–May 1997, 14.

## Chapter 17: Sharing the Joys

1. Adapted from Karen Norheim, "The Art of Giving and Receiving," in *Mrs. Preacher: Succeeding as a Minister's Wife: For Those in the Parsonage and the Pew* (Joplin, Mo.: College Press, 1985), 103–7.

2. Paul Meier, Frank Minirth et al., *What They Didn't Teach You in Seminary* (Nashville: Nelson, 1993), 227–28.

## Chapter 18: Sharing the Wealth

1. For further reading, see Mary Hunt, *The Complete Cheapskate* (Colorado Springs: Focus on the Family, 1997).

2. Dolphus Weary and William Hendricks, *I Ain't Comin' Back* (Wheaton, Ill.: Tyndale House, 1993), 22.

## Chapter 19: Open the Door with Grace and Say Good-Bye

1. Norris Smith, foreword to *Beyond Termination,* by Myra Marshall with Dan McGee and Jennifer Bryon Owen (Nashville: Broadman, 1990), viii. Norris Smith is a Forced Termination Consultant with the Sunday School Board of the Southern Baptist Convention.

2. Ibid., 113.

3. Ibid., 114.